AF520678

Kargil Blunder

Pakistan's Plight, India's Victory

Attention Authors

Manas Publications is fighting a war to tell the world that India can win the battle not only by bullet but also by pen. We are converting fighters into writers as there is no dearth of intellectuals in our country but their knowledge is confined to them only. No sincere effort has been made by any other publisher to give right direction to their knowledge and the talent of every intellectual is lying hidden. An author always gives the raw material in the shape of manuscript and it depends on a publisher that how to make it a finished product. We are motivating the intellectuals' mind and publishing their manuscripts for more than two decades and would like to publish your manuscript, too. If you or your colleagues have any manuscript or are working on it, please don't hesitate to contact us with detailed synopsis and contents, for its publication. We take utmost care in production and give wide publicity to the book and its author. We can also suggest you the title related to your subject for writing, as we are the publishers who believe more in quality than in quantity.

Kargil Blunder

Pakistan's Plight, India's Victory

Major General Y. Bahl (Retd.)
AVSM, SC

Manas Publications
New Delhi - 110 002 (India)

MANAS PUBLICATIONS
(We Convert Fighters into Writers)
(Publishers, Library Suppliers, Importers & Exporters)
4402/5-A, Ansari Road (Opp. HDFC Bank)
Darya Ganj, New Delhi-110 002 (India)
Off. 23260783, 23265523, Fax: 011-23272766
E-mail: manaspublications@gmail.com
manaspublications@yahoo.com

© **Maj. Gen. Y. Bahl**

ISBN 81-7049-120-7

Third Impression 2015

₹ 495/-

All rights reserved. This book is sold subject to the condition that it shall not, by way of trade or otherwise, be lent, resold, hired out, or otherwise circulated, without the publisher's prior written consent, in any form of binding, soft cover or e-version, etc. except by the authorised companies and without a similar condition including this condition being imposed on the subsequent purchaser and without limiting the rights under copyright reserved above, no part of this publication may be reproduced, stored in or introduced into a retrieval system, or transmitted in any form or by any means (electrical, mechanical, photocopying, recording or otherwise) without the prior written permission of the publisher of the book.

Cataloguing/listing of this book for re-sale purpose can be done only by the authorised companies. Cataloguing/listing or sale by unauthorised distributors/bookshops/booksellers, etc. is strictly prohibited and will be legally prosecuted.

The views expressed and suggestions made are those of the author in his personal capacity and do not have any official endorsement. The publisher is not responsible for the views of the author and authenticity of the data, in any way whatsoever.

All disputes are subject to Delhi jurisdiction only.

Designed at
Manas Publications

Printed in India at
RK Offsets, Delhi
and Published by Mrs Suman Lata for
Manas Publications, 4402/5-A, Ansari Road
Darya Ganj, New Delhi-110 002 (INDIA)

Preface

As was the case in 1947-48; 1965; 1971 and now in 1999, the often expected pattern of vert and covert military activity, the intrusion of armed guerrillas (including foreign mercenaries) culminating in an offensive was again staged in Kashmir in may'99. This happened at a time when serious peace efforts were being undertaken (Lahore Declaration), and may be, the Kashmir issue could have been put in a deep freeze by converting the LOC into an international border. This was scuttled by the military junta with, may be, the reluctant concurrence of the rulers.

The uncoordinated intelligence system, a mindset which did not see and believe an offensive, a complascent attitude of the army and a 'no war' scene coupled with concentration on the internal security and anti terrorism, resulted in Pakistan achieving total surprise. Pakistan thereby occupied tactically important heights in Kargil, Batalik and Drass thereby disrupting the Srinagar - Leh high way which could have choked the life line to Siachen. This precisely was the Pakistani strategic aim.

Once the reality dawned the Indian army fought bravely and slowly but surely, despite harsh terrain and qualitative deficiencies of equipment. The army commenced retaking lost territories and restored the adverse situation. Good junior leadership, determination of troops, useful air operations though to a limited extent due to various limitations, innovative use of artillery and the role of media resulted in victory both militarily as well as diplomatically. The facade put up by the Pakistani army and its government, that it was the mujahideen which were fighting was dismantled very soon as the events disclosed. There is a need to seriously ponder over the lapses at the senior leadership level in the army and the government.

Nawaz Sharif's trip to Washington on 4th July (American Independence Day) and being told to withdraw from Indian territory was at a time when the tide had already turned and ninty percent of recapture was already achieved. This climb down by Pakistan was not only an acceptance of its violation of LOC but also a great embarrassment within the country. This caused internal dissent and was the cause of the downfall of Sharif government on 12th Oct. 1999.

For India, which despite great provocations withheld its option of opening another front and thereby exercised restraint, it was a moral victory and acclaimed world wide. Military victory mature media coverage coupled with excellent diplomatic battle was the reasons for the rise in the stature of India in the eyes of International Community.

A stable Pakistan is in India's interest and India should play it's role without compromising its position on Kashmir to see a stable Pakistan.

The 'Operation Vijay' at Kargil has been covered in this book by putting together the views of various experts from different fields so that the readers get a complete all round picture.

The book gives a complete overview of all facets of the battle and as perceived by various athors.

Major General Y. Bahl

The Contributors

Major General Afsir Karim, AVSM (Retd.) belongs to the Parachute Regiment of the Indian Army. He has also served at all levels of his professional career including command of an Infantry Brigade on the Line of Control and as Major General Operational Logistics in the Northern Army.

Arun Bhagat was Director, Intelligence Bureau (IB) of India. He has also served as Commissioner of Police, Delhi Police.

Major General Y. Bahl, AVSM, SC retired as MGGS from Headquarter Northern Command, Udhampur (J&K).

Jaswant Singh is the Minister of External Affairs, India

Mohan Guruswamy is well known defence and media analyst. He has also served as adviser to Finance Minister of India.

Air Cmde. N.B. Singh retired as Director Operations (Air Defence) at Air HQ, New Delhi. He was also Dy. Director and Editor of United Service Institution (USI), New Delhi. His latest book `AIR POWER IN THE NEW MILLENNIUM has just been published by Manas Publications.

Parvez Dewan, an IAS officer of Jammu & Kashmir state cadre, is at present Commissioner/Secretary,

Tourism, Jammu & Kashmir Government. His latest book `PARVEZ DEWAN'S JAMMU, KASHMIR & LADAKH is under print with the Manas Publications.

S.K. Singh retired as Foreign Secretary of India. He was also Indian Ambassador in Pakistan.

Lt. Gen. Vijay Madan, PVSM, VSM (Retd.) is from Infantry and has been the Commandant, College of Combat, Mhow (MP), which is a think tank of the army.

Vijay Naik is a senior journalist and at present Chief of Bureau, Sakal Group of Paper. His latest book `SOUTH AFRICA: The Land of Mandela has just been released by the Hon'ble Vice President of India which has published by Manas Publications.

Introdouction

The misadventure launched in Kargil by Pakistan in 1999 has been reviewed by a large number of historians, journalists, military strategists and observers. Historically and in particular after the partition of India, this area has occupied a strategic position and has therefore been the cause of this latest intrusion by Pakistan. The spin-offs from this action by Pakistan, slow initial response and later an excellent reaction by the Indian Army and of course the commendable diplomatic battle, has been felt in terms of military strategies, political environment, global positions, and geo political angles and hence needs detailed examination. Various observers and researchers of history have elucidated the story in terms of their views and which merit close study. These are given in the succeeding pages to give an overview, analysis, and genesis of the problem and likely course that the situation may take.

Contents

1

Kargil-Historical Perspective

Parvez Dewan

Much of present day Kargil district was once known as Purig. The region called Purig included the areas around Kargil town, the Suru valley, Shagh(k)ar, Chiktan, Pashk(y)um, Bodh Kharbu and Mulbek(h).

We have almost nothing to go by when we try to study the history of Purig (pronounced pu-reeg). However, the 20th century historians Moulvi Hashmat Ullah Khan and Kachu Sikandar Khan[1] have been able to piece together a fairly satisfactory history. They have mostly relied on oral sources- and some references contained in Tibetan chronicles. Of course, 'satisfactory' means, sometimes accepting dates accurate to the nearest 1200 years.

The name 'Purig': There are three theories about the name Purig itself. One is that it is a contraction of the Tibetan phrase 'pot reeks', which means 'of Tibetan origin'. It probably dates to the era when a Tibetan dynasty first established a government in most of Purig. Another interpretation is that Purig means 'tube' and refers to the tubular valleys that make up the inhabited parts of the region. Scholars like Francke feel that the word has been derived from 'burig', which means 'the brave race'. The 'race' in question is the Dards.

The ancient period the early settlers: Dard and Lone

Human habitation seems to have been late in coming to this incredibly cold and rugged district-perhaps as late as 500 BC (Dras, for instance, is the world's second coldest, inhabited place, after Siberia). The Dards of the various little valleys of Gilgit were perhaps the first to settle here. They belonged to the so-called Aryan 'race'. (Gilgit is in Dardistan, now in POK). The Dards traveled to Kargil through Baltistan and Deosai, some of them staying on in Baltistan itself.

The Dards ruled over Purig till the Tibetan attack on Zanskar- and the Tibetan rule that followed in Purig. (When did the attack on Zanskar take place? Moulvi Hashmat Ullah Khan says 180 BC. Kachu Sikandar Khan says 9th or 10th century AD. But then, what's 11 or 12 centuries between friends?)

The language, customs, racial characteristics and religious practices of the Dards can still be found in some areas like Da- Hanu and Chiktan- Garkun, and to some extent in Shanghu- Shaghar. However, by and large, most of the Dards- including some of their most ancient tribes- got assimilated with the Tibetans.

(The Government of India had, in the 1970s restricted the entry of tourists into the Da- Hanu area. This was partly to preserve the purity and antiquity of these 'Aryan' practices and partly because the area had begun to attract neo- Nazis. Several (Western) guidebooks have written about the incident that triggered off this ban. Around 1976 two young (West

German women landed up in Da Hanu to receive the seed of this '100% pure Aryan stock'. However, in 1993, in my first stint as Secretary (Tourism) of the state, I was able to get the ban lifted for one half of this area.)

The Dards were not the first people to settle in Shanghu- Shaghar and Drass. The pioneers here were the seven sons of Pois Lone. They came over from the Chalaas region (near Nanga Parbat) through Deosai. Members of this clan spread all over the Kharmang valley (Baltistan, POK). They mostly settled in the Barsachal, Targon and Tarkati villages. Their culture and language are different from that of the Dards of, say, Da-Hanu or Garkun.

The Dards of Da- Hanu etc. migrated there from the Yanding and Sachal areas of ancient Gilgit. Their language, Brushaski, is the same as that spoken in the fabled Hunza valley (also in POK). Hunza is considered the original Shangri La by many because of the very high life expectancy of the region.

The early Dards spread right up to Khaltse, Rong Chhorgyot and Skandang in Leh district. Within the Dards there seems to have been a core group that controlled all of Purig till the Tibetan conquest. This group owed nominal allegiance to Kashmir.

Migration from Central India

Around the same period a handful of people from central India, too, migrated to Purig. They rapidly assimilated with the Dards. Dastak Paldan and Seergaya Motik led them. (Sikandar Khan feels that the latter name corresponds to the Sanskrit Suryamati.)

Apparently they set up their first colony in a cave in the Shakolchey hill near the Dodu hamlet of present day

Pashkum. They constructed a house in Maazanthang. The house came to be known as Sargyamotik-khar. They also constructed canals in Khurbathang- the very place being developed for agriculture even today- and Saskot.

Around the same time (the eighth century AD according to Sikandar) Lama Naropar and Guru Urgyen Padmaa (Padmaa*n*, actually) came from Zanskar. They took Seergaya Motik and Dastak Paldan with them to Kashmir. Kargili historians like Kachu Sikandar claim that these four 'established the first human habitation in Kashmir, at Pampore, this being the era in which the great lakes of Kashmir were being drained and habitable land was emerging on their beds'.

Now, this does seem a bit too much. I have no problems with accepting that the first humans in Kashmir might have come from Kargil and Zanskar. Nor even that these four could have been the saints referred to in Kashmir's own histories as the first humans to have lived there. However, by the eighth century AD we have evidence of a sophisticated civilisation in Kashmir. We have precise details beginning 1184 BC about which king ruled Kashmir when, and for how many years, months and *days*. Therefore, even Hashmat Ullah's 120 BC seems late by a thousand years.

However, it is possible that it was Seergaya Motik who constructed the fort near the Indus River in Stakna (Leh).

Later, some people migrated to Purig from Leh. Among them were Tisok and Gangasok, who were considered goddesses by some. They built a fort on the Tolon hill near the Indus. Sikandar says that they were Dards but according to Hashmat they were Mons. They also founded the Achinathang village. Ruins of that ancient settlement can still be found. This fort was then called the Tolonkhar. It was later taken over by the rulers of Chiktan, who also founded the Stakshan hamlet.

Tisok- Gangasok, and their colleagues Cho Paldan and Chocho Kunzum, decided to settle in Stakchey[2]. At that stage all of Purig was ruled by the Dards. The Tibetans controlled only Kateeka Phokar. (The house the 'goddesses' and their colleagues got constructed at Chiktan Khar was later subsumed by a 16th century AD building. However, on the ground floor there is an ancient, decaying window that is said to have been a part of the original.)

Historians like Kachu Sikandar feel that the history of Purig/ Kargil is really the history of these two dynasties and clans: the Dards and the Tibetans. For reasons of brevity we will only look at the fortunes of the central section of Kargil, leaving out the branches.

The story of Shaghar- Chiktan and Sot- Pashkum Gasho Thatha Khan

In the eighth (or maybe early ninth) century AD, Gasho Thatha Khan started the dynasty that would rule over the Shakar and Chiktan area for almost a thousand years. He was a scion of the royal family of Gilgit (now in POK).

There are two theories about him. One is that he was an infant child when hunters found him atop a hillock. When he reached manhood they made him their king, to replace the cruel man who was ruling over them. An oracle had told the unpopular king about the man who would one day wrest his throne from him. Since the description fitted Thatha Khan, the king ordered his assassination.

The other tradition speaks of a Gilgit prince called Thakan whom his stepbrother Shri Bagor Tham wanted killed. This led to a civil war between the supporters of the two brothers. ('Thakan' looks suspiciously like a contraction of 'Thatha Khan'.'Shri' is a part of the latter's name.)

Either way, the story goes, our friend Thatha was sitting in a large hall watching a dance. Thatha's rival, the king, sent his men to kill him. The king thought that Thatha would be too busy enjoying himself to be able to resist the soldiers.

However, the musicians, who loved Thatha, got to know of the plot. They started singing a song that warned him of the impending attack. Thatha pulled out his sword and planted it firmly in the ground. He then stepped on the hilt of his sword to reach the chimney, through which he escaped.

(Sounds like something out of a classical opera, what? Well, that's how the story traveled down over more than a thousand years. 'Remembrancers' sing out such epic stories, serialised over a week of dinners around a brazier, in the winters, after snow has blocked the passes and there's little else to do. This way history gets mixed with folklore, but it is all we have to go by.)

Thatha travels through Kargil

Thatha fled to Baltistan (also now in POK). He was accompanied by his 'milk father' Saati Tam and his 'milk brother' Booti Tam. (Milk- brothers are men who have shared the same wet nurse or foster mother.) They entered Kargil through the Chhurbat La (pass). On the banks of the Indus river they found an uninhabited bur fertile place, with a natural spring. There was no bridge to cross the river on. However, since the river was frozen they walked across on the ice. Thatha had a walnut seed in his pocket, which he planted there.

They next went to Kokashu, which, too, they noticed was fertile. The staff Thatha carried had been taken from a *bhoj* tree and was still green. He planted it in the centre of the plains of Kokashu.

The three decided not to settle in any of these uninhabited villages. They sought the waters of the Indus at Chey Chey Thang. After that they went to Blargo where cats sitting on a rock welcomed them with a dance. A wealthy Brokpa had already settled there and had erected a tower of rakibis.

Their next stop was Brolmo. There a senior female citizen warned them of the man- eating 'lion' that lived in the rocky mountains of Kharol, at the point where the Drass and Suru rivers met. She also taught Thatha how to kill this animal, which he did. (Whether it is Jammu, Kashmir or Ladakh, in all three regions they use just one word to describe all big cats. They have the same word for lion, panther, tiger, cheetah, leopard etc. I suspect this one must have been a leopard.)

Tales of Thatha's bravery spread throughout the land. These stories continue to be told to this day. In particular, his moustaches inspired fear and awe among the people. (Not just in Kargil but in most of North India rural people seem to be fond of ferocious looking rulers.)

After that our heroes went to Sot, where a wealthy Dard clan called Sot Saaral gave them jobs. The older man was employed as a tiller and the two youths as shepherds. (Sot rhymes with 'coat', except that the 't' is soft.) Thatha once told his boss of a dream he had seen.

The employer interpreted it as indication, that one day Thatha would be the emperor.

After a while the three returned to Kokashu and **Dargo**. The bhoj and walnut had by then grown into mature trees. (These trees would later grow into full-fledged forests, which exist to this day. The tree that Thatha had planted remained there till Zorawar Singh's time (around 1850). The spot where it had stood has been marked with stones.) Thatha considered this a good omen. He got a house constructed at each, Totokhar for himself and Patokhar for the other two.

One day the trio climbed the peak of the Neen Dum hill. From there they could see parts of Drass in the west, the Suru Valley in the south, and the Indus Valley and Khaltse in the east. They prayed that someday they should rule it all. Before long they did.

Thatha becomes the king

During Thatha's reign several people migrated to Purig/ Kargil. The first was the Ahmed-pa family. (Interesting name). It helps fix dates. It indicates that these events took place after the founding of Islam.) Then came Tisok and Gangasok. These 'goddesses' were given the house in Chiktan mentioned above and over which area they later ruled, if briefly.

The other contemporary sovereigns who then ruled in what is now Kargil district were Cho Paldan and Chocho Kunzum.

From well before this era, the people of Turkmenistan were in the habit of attacking and raiding the Mon rulers of upper Ladakh. This time they took Tisok- Gangasok, Cho Paldan and Chocho Kunzum back with them as hostages. Thatha moved into the vacuum that was thus created and added their territories to his.

Sot and other principalities are united

The ruler of Sot found himself caught between two aggressive, expansionist powers- the minority Tibetans and the majority Dards. He realised that he couldn't resist both- or even either. So, he simply handed his kingdom over to Thatha.

Now, many of Thatha's supporters in Gilgit started migrating to Sot. Thatha shifted his capital to Kokashu and built his palace where the former ruler's house had stood.

After establishing power in Sot, Thatha diverted his attention to development. He got forests cleared to establish Kargil and Poeen Shalkchey, where he persuaded people from Ladakh and Skardu to settle. (In that age the clearing of forests was considered an achievement.) Kargil was named after its pioneer, a noble called Kargeel. Thatha also established Oma Chak Thang, where his descendants still own land. After that he gradually brought Baru, Manji and Gund under his control. In time so were the Dard rulers of Khaltse.

Thatha then established Trespon (lit. 'the village of djinns'). I have a particular fascination for the grand Imam Bara (Shiite place of worship) of Trespon- because of its spiritual power as well as its picturesque hilltop location and colourful architecture. Ruins of what Thatha built can still be seen at Seemo Khar, near the Imam Bara.

He next turned to Suru- Karchey, which were then ruled by the Tibetans. Their capital was at Phokar. The Tibetans' administration had begun to show signs of decay. Thatha assigned this area to his son, Navaldey. In turn, Navaldey sent his son Chorazi Astan to establish an autonomous principality there, with its capital at present day Sangra. Their dynasty came to an end a few generations later, with the immensely popular ruler, Aldey Choo.

(Navaldey's eldest brother Boti Khan alias Moi Gasho was granted the main Sot- Shaghar- Chiktan territory. Their third brother was settled in Gund.)

Thus, according to 9th century folksongs, did Thatha subdue and annex independent principalities. This was at a time when the ancient Dard Empire was crumbling but the Tibetans were in the ascendant in Baltistan and lower Ladakh, and in power in Purig (Kargil). However, as historian Sikandar Khan puts it, after Thatha, the Dard, established his new kingdom, 'the Tibetans no longer had the courage to interfere' (in Purig).

Thatha's successors: AD 825- 1050

Dates start getting somewhat clearer after Thatha's reign. However, even now they are only approximate, and have been rounded to the nearest half- decade.

Thatha's son Boti Khan had an eventless reign (circa AD 825 to 850). He seems to have been a contemporary of Nemagon. (See 'A history of Leh'.) The next five rulers were equally colourless.

Jadeem Beig (c. 975- 1000) was the eighth king of the dynasty. He conquered Lama Yuru, Bodh Kharbu, Lingshit, Vanla, Stakchey and Kanji, extending his kingdom to the Khaltse Bridge. Apparently Khaltse was partitioned between (or ruled by both) the Sot and Khaltse rulers: both kings collected taxes in Khaltse.

Drass had hitherto been loosely subject to Kashmir. Jadeem's son Abdula (c.1000-1025) conquered the Drass area, right upto the Dzoji La pass. He met with no resistance, because the people of the area were mostly fellow Dards.

The spread of Buddhism

A significant development during the reign of Abdal's grandson Chhabzang Cho (c. 1060-1090) was the spread of Buddhism. Lama Losava Rinchen Zangpo was going back from the Indian plains to his native Guge (Western Tibet). He preached the Buddhist gospel wherever he passed. He got Lha Khangs (Buddhist temples; Lha= God) constructed at Chiktan and Wakha (near Mulbek). It is believed that it was he who got the stone idol of Chamba Devi built at Mulbek.

The medieval era

The advent of Islam

The next important era is that of Amrood Cho, also known as Mureed Khan (c.1450- 1475). This was when Islam first spread in Purig, through the efforts of the saint Ameer Kabeer Syed Ali Hamdani and his disciple Syed Muhammad Noor Baksh. That the ruler had an alternate, Islamic, name seems to indicate that he, too, had converted to Islam, or followed two religions (as twelve per cent of India does even today). Khan, incidentally, is *not* an Islamic surname. (Genghis, to take a particularly celebrated example, was not a Muslim.)

The 15th century: Disintegration

The people gave Amrood's elder son and successor Dooroo Cho the nickname Ald-dor Cho, meaning the 'lax and incompetent one'. He was cruel as well. Not surprisingly, under him the administrative structure of the state collapsed.

So, the Gyapo of Tingmo(s)gang annexed the areas between the Khaltse bridge and the Kanji nallah. The king of Astor, possibly Maqpon Shah Sultan, helped himself to Drass. Gyalbom Aldey Raja Phokar took Suru and Karchey (Kartse). That left just Chiktan and Sot with Dooroo. His angry subjects punished him for his incompetence. They ensured that he was allowed to eat only half as much as he used to before. (He was under some kind of house arrest.)

Dooroo died childless. He was succeeded by his younger brother Habib Cho (c. 1490 to 1510). During Habib's reign Mir Shams ud Din, propagated Islam-especially the Imamiya or Shia school, in Purig and Baltistan.The Mir was a saint from Iraq and a disciple of Syed Muhammad Noor Baksh. Habib Cho accepted Shia (Shiite) doctrines. His father had already converted to Islam.

Habib allied with the kings of Khaplu, Shaghar and Skardu. Together they attacked Leh, in order to recover the territory Dooroo had lost to the Gyapos. The Gyapo agreed to pay a heavy tribute. However, this tribute was paid mostly to the King of Shaghar, and not to the other three allies.

Habib's son Ahmed Malik Khan (c. 1510- 1535) succeeded him. During his reign, Sultan Saeed Waai, who was a Turkmen, attacked Leh, Zanskar, Suru and Sot. (He also invaded Kashghar and Kashmir.) Ahmed accepted the Sultan's superiority.

The Turkmens must have stayed in Purig for a while, because they left some major landmarks behind. Among them is the Hor Lam, the Turkmen road that runs between Gund, Mangalpur and Selskot. The Turkmens left a deep imprint on the culture of Ladakh- including its songs and folk- tales. (In this context a Turkmen really means a Mughal directly from Central Asia, rather than from Delhi- Agra.)

The ambitious Sarang Malik

Khokhor Baghram (c.1535- 1555) inherited the throne from his father Ahmed. He made friends with Gyapo Tsewang Namgyal in order to buy peace for his eastern borders. His younger son Sarang Malik was the governor of Chiktan. Sarang was an ambitious young man. A bit too ambitious. He wanted to be the king. He started going to the court of Gyapo Jamyang Namgyal.

Now Jamyang fancied Sarang's wife. So, Sarang divorced her and handed her over to Jamyang, who made an honest woman of her. She is best known by the hybrid name Sarang Rigyalmo (lit: Queen Mother Sarang). The historian Maulvi Hashmatullah says that she was pregnant (presumably by Jamyang himself) when she married the Gyapo. The child thus born was Lhwang Namgyal.

The sordidness didn't end there. In exchange, Jamyang gave his own daughter in marriage to Sarang, promised to help him and asked him to go home. Jamyang was happy that he had now obtained a foothold in Purig.

According to tradition, en route the Gyapo got Sarang imprisoned at Matho and Sarang's new queen at Stok. Sarang's supporters resorted to arms, attacked Leh and got the royal couple freed. Subsequently perhaps the Gyapo and Sarang patched up.

On his return to Purig, Sarang declared Chiktan independent. This could have led to a civil war between Sarang and his brother Rigyal Malik. Their father, Khokhor Baghram, acted wisely and saved the kingdom from ruination by partitioning it between the two.

Around this time, Ali Sher Khan, the heir apparent of Skardu, conquered parts of Baltistan. In those days the Gyapo of Leh would post a representative (a 'resident' of sorts), as well as soldiers, at Kartakhsha (Baltistan). Ali Sher personally chased both the Resident and the soldiers out of Baltistan.

Now, Sarang controlled the Chiktan area and Rigyal the Sot area. Relations between the two were tense. Sarang, ever the ambitious one, got in touch with Ali Sher. Ali attacked Sot and, thus, formalised Chiktan's independence. In return, Sarang gifted Bodh Kharbu and some neighbouring villages to Ali Sher. Ali stationed his soldiers at the Bodh Kharbu fort and left. On its way home his army burnt and destroyed several Ladakhi villages.

An enraged Jamyang Namg11yal and his army suddenly showed up at Bodh Kharbu. They had traveled through the Fatu La. It was a Friday. The Balti soldiers were offering prayers at Chhorbas Spang. The people of Bodh Kharbu were Buddhists, like Jamyang. They helped him seize the Bodh Kharbu fort. The area was thus liberated from Ali Sher.

The Gyapo received Sarang at Bodh Kharbu. He wasn't particularly angry with his son in law. He even allowed Sarang to retain his independence.

Just then Ali Sher was told about the defeat of his soldiers. He allied with Balti princes and attacked Leh.

So, Jamyang had to rush back. (See also 'Losar' in the chapter on 'The Buddhist Festivals of Leh and Zanskar'.)

In the event, both Jamyang and Sarang retained their thrones, and kept their kingdoms intact. Indeed, Sarang added Pashkum to his territories, by intervening in a dispute that centred on a love affair. Encouraged by his closeness to the Gyapo, he also annexed villages like Skambo Yocham, Kostey, Tacha Karat, Kargil, Baru, Manji and Kannaur. These villages had thitherto been under Pashkum.

Sot, Pashkum and Chiktan are united- for a while

Sultan Malik (c.1600- 1610) inherited from his father Rigyal Malik both the thrones of Sot and the grudge against Sarang. He attacked and annexed Chiktan and Pashkum. Sarang and his son Sankhan fought bravely, but both were killed. Sultan imprisoned Sankhan's minor sons Adam and Chhosaraang Mailk at Yukma Kharbu.

Most of the people of Chiktan were Buddhists. Some of them were related by blood to the kings of Leh. They started agitating against the people of, and control by, Sot. They sent a delegation to Ali Sher Khan, who, by then, was the Maqpon of Skardu. They also contacted Senge Namgyal of Leh, who did not seem interested in helping them.

Ali Sher did.

In those days there lived in Skardu a doctor from Chiktan. His name was Chhozaang Kashi. He had cured Ali Sher's queen of some disease. Instead of a reward all he asked of Ali Sher was that the delegation from Chiktan be listened to sympathetically. The Maqpon did just that. He even sent his vizier and nobles to Sultan Malik, who freed the two minor princes.

Under pressure from the Baltis of Skardu, Sultan even restored Adam to his ancestral throne. Once again Pashkum and Chiktan became independent of Sot.

Now Senge Namgyal attacked Purig, ostensibly to avenge the then recent invasion of Chiktan. He wrested Wakha and Mulbek and, after a while, Kartsey (Karchey) and Suru from different kings.

Senge then prepared to attack Sot. Sultan Muhammad (c.1610- 1650), the son of Sultan Malik, was the King of Sot by then. He sought the help of Skardu's Adam Khan. At Adam Khan's request, Ali Mardan Khan, the Mughal governor of Kashmir, sent a detachment of the Mughal army to help out Purig.

The Mughal- Balti force met Senge at Karpokhar. By most accounts- at least according to the credible ones- the Mughals won. Thus Suru and Karchey were freed from the control of Leh. However, Wakha and Mulbek continued to remain under Leh. (So, the historians of Leh were at least partly right when they claimed that the Leh army had defeated the Mughal- Balti combine.)

The Kargilis believe that when the Turkmens (Mughals) invaded Kargil at Pasri Khar, Muhammad Sultan repulsed their attack- in alliance with the Leh army. (So, the historians of Leh (and Bhaderwah) are not alone in claiming victory over the Mughals for their kings.)

This was the first time that the Mughals of Delhi-Agra had sent their forces into Ladakh.

The last independent kings

Muhammad Sultan's son Mirza Sultan (c.1650- 1660) was the next king of Sot. Mirza Sultan's throne, in turn, passed on to his descendants Mirza Beig, Baghram Beig, Jangeer Beig and Yahya Khan, in that order.

If folk- songs are to be believed, then of all these kings, Arbab Shah was the best. Peace and prosperity marked his reign. During Baghram Khan's tenure, Sot and Karchey allied against Leh. Together they captured Kharol, Chhotok and some neighbouring villages. However, some influential people of Sot were secretly working for the Gyapo of Leh. The Gyapo launched a counter- attack with their help. Baghram Khan had to surrender the gains he had made only recently.

Yahya Khan (c.1780- 1810) succeeded his father Jangeer Beig. His mother was perhaps the sister of the king of Karchey. His son, Salaam Khan (1810- 1834) was the next- and last- king of Sot. It was during Salaam's reign that the Dogras conquered Purig, Baltistan and Leh.

The modern age the Dogra conquest

In the summer of 1834, Maharaja Gulab Singh of Jammu sent Zorawar Singh, his legendary army chief, to annex Ladakh.

Officially Gulab was conquering Ladakh for his Maharaja. However, he sought (and received) the blessings of the British to add Ladakh to Jammu. An alarmed king of Ladakh sent numerous messages to the British that he would ally with them. He was ignored.

Zorawar's army traveled to Ladakh through Kishtwar and Zanskar.

Ladakh did not then have a proper army: just a civil defence system. At Sankoo in Kargil's Suru valley volunteers got together and offered some resistance.

The Dogra army brushed them aside. By the time the invaders reached Pashkum Kargil's dreaded winter announced itself. The Dogras of the scorching plains of Jammu sent word to the king of Leh that they would withdraw if he would pay them Rs.15,000. The king rejected the offer, on his wife's advice.

Snubbed, Zorawar retreated to a place near Sankoo, where his army and he decided to camp for the winter, biding their time. The Ladakhi army waited till the next April to attack Zorawar's men. The Ladakhis were defeated.

Kargil joins Kashmir and Jammu

The Dogras appointed Salaam Khan, the defeated king, as the chief administrator of the areas over which his father- and their ancestors before that had ruled. (His descendants continued to occupy senior positions in the government even in the second half of the twentieth century, after the state acceded to India.)

The fortunes of Purig, indeed of all Kargil, now merged with those of Leh and Jammu. Soon Kashmir would join the lot. Therefore, the history of Kargil after that would substantially be the same as that of Leh, Kashmir or Jammu.

In independent India

In August 1947, as soon as Pakistan came into being, it wanted to annex 'Jammu and Kashmir', the multi-ethnic state the Dogras had forged together. So, on the 22nd October, the Pakistani army sent irregular tribal soldiers into Kashmir- including Kargil, The state acceded to India on the 26th October 1947. The

Pakistani army captured Baltistan, Skardu, Gilgit, Hunza etc, which it now administers under the name 'the Northern Areas'. It denies these Areas political representation, despite directions from its own Supreme Court.

In every war with Pakistan, the people of Kargil have supported India, for which they have paid a heavy price. During each war, and often in peacetime as well, their towns and villages have been shelled by the Pakistani army, which is stationed on hilltops overlooking Kargil.

In 1998, Pakistan fired rockets from its side of the line of control several hundred times. It would routinely shell vehicles travelling on the Kargil section of the national highway. It also destroyed the Kargil district hospital, an upmarket hotel and, more ominously, two Shia mosques. I don't believe that even Sunni Pakistan would deliberately have tried to destroy Shia mosques. But during the 1999 war the Pakistani army officially boasted of the accuracy of its artillery. Does that mean that the mosques had been targeted, and not hit by mistake?

The Kargil War

In May 1999, Pakistan dragged Kargil into the international limelight by capturing some territory and shelling several towns and villages. This forced much of Kargil town to relocate to places outside the range of Pakistan's artillery.

In the proceeding months, around 1,500 Pakistanis had infiltrated into Indian Territory in Mashkoh Valley, Drass, Kaksar and Batalik. According to the Pakistani press, their aim was to dominate the National Highway between Srinagar and Leh and, thus, cut Siachen and Leh off from Srinagar.

The battle to liberate the territory captured by the Pakistanis lasted 74 days (May-July, 1999), during which 407 Indians and 696 Pakistanis were killed. *India Today* estimates that the war cost India Rs.1,110 crore ($250 million). Pakistan's finance minister put the cost to his country at $700 million.

Pakistan has officially claimed, and several times at that, that the motive behind its intrusion was to 'internationalise' the Kashmir issue and that Pakistan had 'succeeded' in doing so. Absolutely. Kashmir was 'internationalised' like never before. On June 20, 1999, eight of the world's richest nations, known as G-8, asked the intruders to withdraw to the Pakistani side of the line of control. They thus gave the LOC the same sanctity as an international border.

China gave its faithful ally, Pakistan, no comfort either. So, the dejected Pakistani Prime Minister, Mr. Nawaz Sharief, rushed to Washington hoping that at least the US would support his country.

The US President, Mr. Bill Clinton, received Mr. Sharief at Blair House- and not the White House- on the Fourth of July. He asked Mr. Sharief to pull the intruders out of Indian Territory immediately. Mr. Sharief complied- well, more or less.

The Pakistani scholar M.P. Bhandara notes that the above mentioned 'Washington Accord [of July 1999 between the US and Pakistan] commits Pakistan to the "inviolability" and "sanctity" of the Line of Control. The use of these strong terms gives the LoC nearly an international- border status. This may not be the way Pakistan interprets it, but this may well be the interpretation of the Security Council members and the world at large." (The *Dawn*, Karachi, Pakistan, August 1999.)

Country after country, including the USA, praised India for its military 'restraint' during the 1999 war, and for not having retaliated by attacking Pakistan.

India had won the war militarily as well as on the diplomatic front.

2

Pakistan's Aggression in Kashmir: 1999

Major General Afsir Karim (Retd.)

Kargil is a small town in Ladakh in Indian Kashmir, which lies on the old caravan route from Tibet to the Kashmir Valley. The caravans carrying Pashmina (a special soft variety of wool), salt and trinkets crossed the Karakoram Pass from Tibet, proceeded to Leh and thereafter to Srinagar via Kargil and Zojila (Zoji pass). This pass, the only negotiable opening in the Great Himalayan Range, which separates the Kashmir Valley from Ladakh, remains snowbound for six months in winter every year. Kargil (and the rest of Ladakh) is cut off from the Kashmir Valley during this period. The Indus valley route from Gilgit – Skardu to Leh, however, remains open for most of the year and can be used by the Pakistan Army even in winter.

Dras, a town near the entrance of Zojila, and Kargil a few miles to the east, remain desolate and deserted throughout the long winter. These habitations come to life again only when Zojila reopens for traffic in summer. The road from Srinagar to Leh crosses Zojila at an elevation of nearly 3,520 m, is one way, with steep gradients.

In the Dras – Kargil area, the armies of India and Pakistan were in eyeball-to eyeball confrontation at several places. The Line of Control in the sector passes uncomfortably close to Zojila, Dras and Kargil. Several Pakistani posts along the LOC overlooked National Highway IA in the Dras – Kargil sector. Artillery barrages from Pakistan to disrupt the supply convoys en route to Leh have been a common feature for the past two years. Armed confrontation across the LOC is not unknown, but the scale of the armed intrusion across the LOC from Pakistan witnessed this year had not taken place even during the 1965 and 1971 wars.

Extensive armed intrusion in Dras, Kargil, Batalik (east of Kargil on the Indus) across the LOC was a new face of the Pakistani offensive which created a warlike situation in Kashmir. The Indian and Pakistani Armies were locked in deadly combat in the high mountains from Dras to Turutuk (a small township on the LOC in Shyok valley south of the Siachen glacier). This was a deliberate and dangerous escalation of hostilities in Kashmir by Pakistan without care for the serious consequences of such action on the future of India – Pakistan relations.

The battles, which raged in Kargil, sector were slow moving but deadly because of extremely difficult mountainous terrain. The ridges here (at elevations of 15-18,000 ft) have very steep gradients, rocky outcrops and craggy tops. A harsh, inhospitable climate with high altitudes where sleet or snow is encountered throughout the year and high-velocity winds blow unceasingly.

The confrontation in Kargil: Summer 1999

In the first week of May 1999, Indian Army formations deployed in Ladakh discovered that Pakistani

forces had crossed the well-established Line of Control (LOC) in Kargil, Batalik, and Chorbat La sectors of western Ladakh. The Pakistani forces were found to be composed of Pak army units, mercenaries and Afghan war veterans. They were well equipped with sophisticated weapons, including Stinger missiles. Pakistani artillery deployed across the LOC supported these elements operating inside the Indian-controlled areas. (Appendix 1.1 shows a sketch of J&K State).

Pakistan's armed presence across the Line of Control is a violation of the Simla Agreement signed in 1972 between India and Pakistan. Violation of this Line by armed forces is, in fact, tantamount to an act of war. By the time the Indian Army got its act together and started an operation to push back the Pak forces across the LOC, the Pakistani forces were already entrenched and had stocked ammunition and ration for three months. The task of evicting well-entrenched troops from the barren mountaintops is a tough one, which can cause a large number of casualties to the assaulting forces.

The main purpose of the Pakistani operation was to enlarge the conflict in Kashmir, and to draw the attention of the international community to the danger of a new Indo-Pak war in which nuclear weapons could be used. By creating this threat, Pakistan hoped for international intervention, which would defreeze the Kashmir situation.

The Pakistani aggression in Kargil sector is the first armed invasion in which Islamic fundamentalists have played a role outside Afghanistan. Pakistan planned to gain major strategic advantages by this action, besides hoping for international intervention. By an offensive in this area, Pakistan wanted to:

Interdict Road Srinagar-Leh to stop movement of supplies to Leh garrison and Siachen through this route.

Block Zojila Pass and threaten Kashmir Valley from the north: a new, unexpected direction.

Control the great Himalayan Range to gain unopposed access for insurgent – terrorists into the Kashmir Valley and Doda district of Jammu.

To outflank the Indian Army deployed on the LOC in northwestern Kashmir and the Siachen glacier through Shyok valley.

No sensible leader in Pakistan should have embarked on such a course owing to a danger of a war in which nuclear weapons could be used. However, fundamentalist forces that hold sway in Pakistan seem to call the shots. These elements have infiltrated the armed forces and other vital organisations of Pakistan. Fundamentalists and fanatics are not expected to be rational, and if they are not controlled, a disastrous situation may soon develop in this region

The situation in the Indian subcontinent can spin out of control if no coordinated international effort is made to rein in the fundamentalist forces, which have emerged after the Afghanistan war. In this context, the USA has to clearly define the meaning and manifestations of Islamic terror and curb the forces of destablilisation let loose by various fundamentalist groups operating from Pakistan.

Title 22 of the United States code section 2656 f (d) defines international terrorism as 'a terrorism involving citizens or the territory of more than one country'. This definition does not specifically cover Islamic terror that exploits religion. Ethnic cleansing of Hindu minorities.

Pakistan's latest aggression in Kargil shows a desire for confrontation and an attitude of belligerence. This attitude is directly connected with the Talibanisation of Pakistani society. The role of Al Qaida, Osama Bin Ladin's organisation, which trains, equips and finances fundamentalist groups is also evident. Al Qaida and several other fundamentalist organisations continue to indoctrinate youths in Pakistan to wage wars against infidels and non-conformist Muslim societies. In return for sanctuaries and safe houses, organisations like Al Qaida provide assistance in training and launching Islamic terrorist groups in Central Asia and Indian Kashmir. The cult of violence propagated by Islamic fundamentalists, easy availability of finances and sophisticated weapons, are factors, which are responsible for Pakistan's aggressive attitude. They have joined the Pakistani armed forces in greater number and fundamentalists enjoy widespread support of the people after the Afghan war.

The current crisis was defused owing to international pressures and the inability of the Pakistani forces to make headway in Kargil. The determined resistance of the Indian Army and repeated military failures in Kargil upset the Pakistani plans. As efforts to disturb peace in Indian Kashmir still continue, the situation can escalate suddenly, particularly if Pakistan persists in sending terrorists across the LOC. In the present circumstances, because of the constraints imposed by the terrain and near parity of the opposing ground forces in Kashmir, overt or covert military confrontation can produce no decisive results. It can only bleed the two countries and cause (avoidable) loss of lives. Pakistan, with its frail economy, may face an economic collapse if it continues the confrontation. In the present conditions, serious internal problems may surface in Pakistan. The dichotomy created by fundamentalist groups in Pakistani society, the growing alienation and belligerence of Mohajirs (Muslim settlers of Indian origin), brutal faction fights between Shias and Sunnis may become unmanageable. Lawlessness and chaos may spread to all corners of Pakistan and political and economic bonds among various states may snap.

Sketch of Jammu & Kashmir State

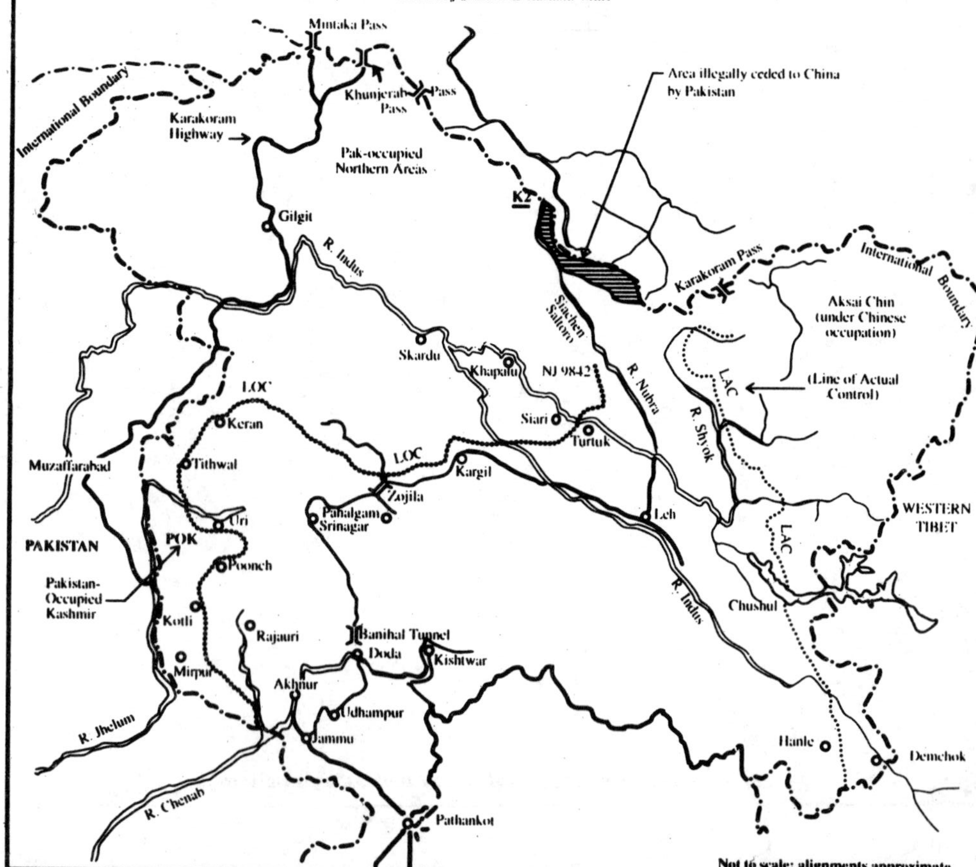

Not to scale; alignments approximate.

Pakistan's Aggression Across the LOC (Kargil Sector): 1999

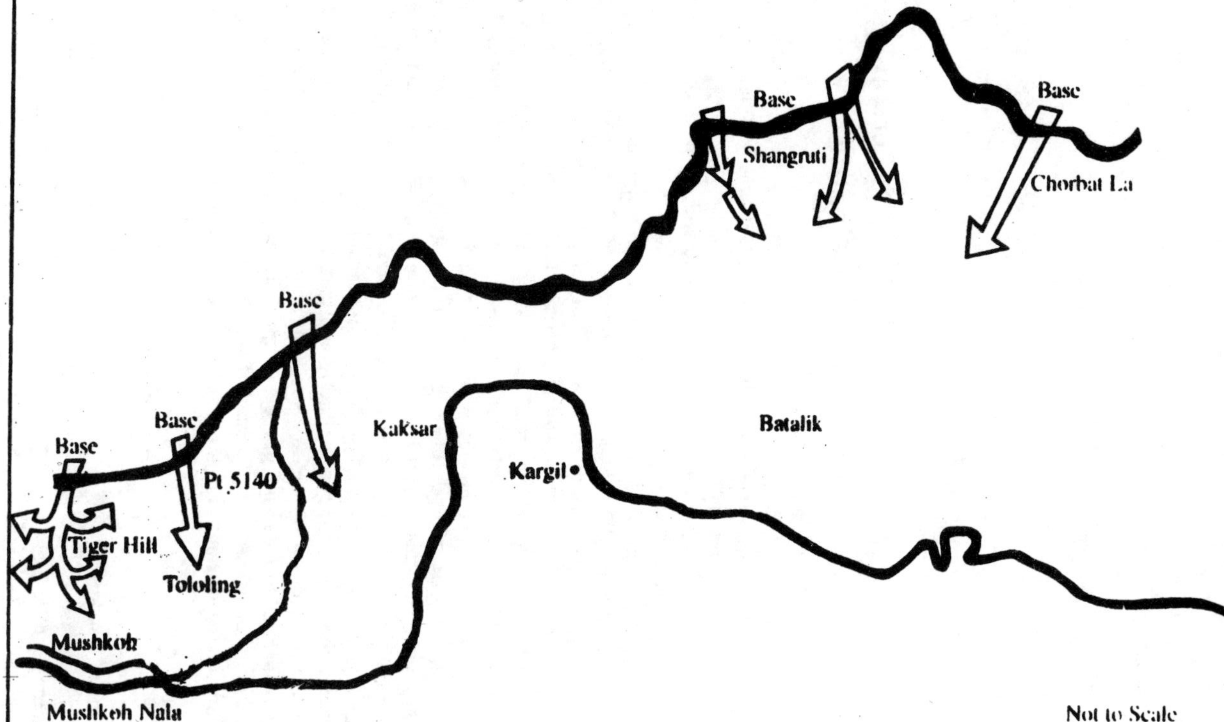

Extract of Simla Agreement Pertaining to the Line Of Control

1 to 3. xxx

4. In order to initiate the process of the establishment of durable peace, both the Governments agree that:

   (i) Indian and Pakistani forces shall be withdrawn to their side of the international border.

   (ii) In Jammu and Kashmir, the line of control resulting from the cease-fire of December, 1971 shall be respected by both sides without prejudice to the recognized position of either side. Neither side shall seek to alter it unilaterally, irrespective of mutual differences and legal interpretations. <u>Both sides further undertake to refrain from the threat or use of force in violation of this Line.</u>

   (iii) The withdrawals shall commence upon entry into force of this Agreement and shall be completed within a period of 30 days thereof.

5. This Agreement will be subject to ratification by both countries in accordance with their respective constitutional procedures, and will come into force with effect from the date on which the Instruments of Ratification are exchanged.

6. Both Governments agree that their respective Heads will meet again at a mutually convenient time in the future and that, in the meanwhile, the representatives of the two sides will meet to discuss further the modalities and arrangements for the establishment of durable peace and normalisation of relations, including the questions of repatriation of prisoners of war and civilian internees, a final settlement of Jammu and Kashmir and the resumption of diplomatic relations.

Sd/- xxx
(Indira Gandhi)
Prime Minister
Republic of India

Sd/- xxx
(Zulfikar Ali Bhutto)
President
Islamic Republic of Pakistan

Simla, the 2nd July, 1972

Delineation of the Line of Control
(Jammu & Kashmir)

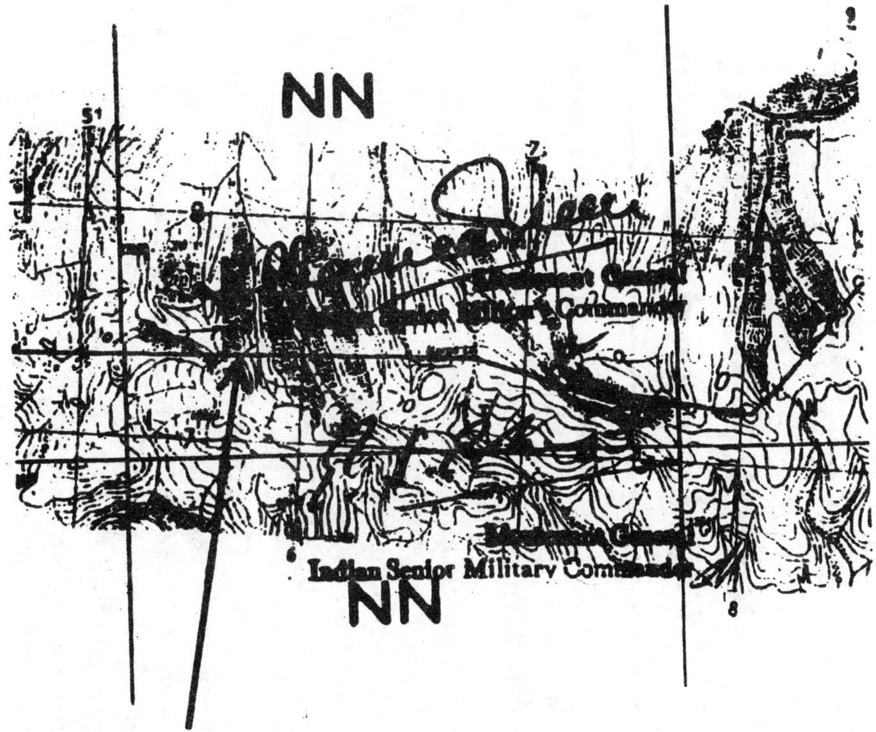

Line of Control

3

Kargil – 99: Before, During and Beyond

Lt. Gen. Vijay Madan (Retd.)

Introduction

A discussion of the recent conflict in Kargil would be stripped of any meaningful content if it does not take into account the genesis of the problem, its current trends and future implications. It would at best be a narration of a battle with very local and limited lessons of a tactical nature only or at worst a mere record of heroic deeds of some individuals and units, as well as critiques of failures of this or that commander and one or the other of the many agencies charged with ensuring national security. Of course some of these subjects, specially the latter ones, must and should figure in any discussion but if restricted only to this particular episode the discussion would lack depth.

Kargil 99 though extremely important in itself, was nevertheless just another of the battles in the war that this country has been fighting over Jammu and Kashmir for over the last fifty-two years. A war whose ultimate result will well decide the future of India- nay the South Asian sub continent itself.

PART-I – SETTING THE STAGE

The most disturbing aspect of Indian Security Planning has been the complete ignorance of the subject of security on the part of those who are "supposed" to deal with this life and death issue of the nation. This was amply demonstrated, if such a demonstration was ever required during the debate in the Parliament after the Pokharan – II nuclear test in 1998. Former Prime Ministers, various members who had adorned the Defence Minister's chair – it may be more appropriate to say who had masqueraded as Defence Ministers; a former Finance Minister who had also once been a Minister of State for Internal Security all asked the same precious question; when did the government realise that the security environment around India had degenerated to the extent that India had to come out in the open as a nuclear weapons power? That was precisely what the Pokharan II tests were all about. It was as if they wanted to know the precise moment the environment changed to India's detriment. They displayed both their gross ignorance of the dynamics, which determine a nation's security environment, as well as their belief that India was otherwise secure and therefore the nuclear tests were uncalled for. The first portion of their question regarding when did India's security environment change adversely can be answered without any hesitation; Indian security environment changed for the worse precisely at the hour of midnight of 14-15 Aug 1947 when India awoke to life and freedom and started the march to keep its tryst with destiny. Since this march was led by none other than Jawaharlal Nehru himself for seventeen long years and subsequently, for the major period of our existence as a free country, by members of his family and his party, the substantial share of the blame for mismanaging India's security lies on their shoulders and their shoulders alone.

As for the perception that India was by and large secure and as such not in the need of any nuclear tests if the possession of more than one third of Jammu and Kashmir by Pakistan; thousands of square Kilometers of that state by China; a savage proxy war in Kashmir from 1990 onwards; terrorism and insurgency in Assam and the other North Eastern states; a Punjab saved after immense sacrifice; nuclear weapons and missiles in India's neighbourhood countries, with one of them India specific only; growing ISI networks inside India ; the rise of Islamic fundamentalism in Pakistan ; an unfriendly turbulent Afghanistan distinctly anti-Indian – the list is unending if all these constitute a reasonable and secure environment in the minds of some of our leaders and parties then we really have no need for enemies. They are already within the country and may soon be within our policy making bodies and the Parliament.

Kargil 99 is one of the offsprings of this degenerated security environment and was fathered by all those in power in this Country since 15 Aug 1947. Of course the question as to when exactly the incursions onto the Kargil heights in 1999 came to the notice of the authorities, military as well as political, is a most relevant one, which needs to be answered unambiguously. Also the question that follows, that why was it not discovered even earlier, as well as what immediate action was taken by the concerned authorities to nip the evil in the bud so to say. An attempt will be made to answer these and related questions in this article. But before that there are host of other questions, which must be asked in order to place Kargil 99 in its correct perspective.

Before Kargil- 99

Many questions remained unanswered. Why did India in Oct 1947, on the insistence of Lord Mountbatten, make the commitment to hold a plebiscite in Jammu and Kashmir, once the Pakistani raiders were cleared from the state? The instrument of accession to India, signed by Maharajah Hari Singh on 25/26 Oct 47, was a perfectly legal document and the Indian Independence Act of the British Parliament, under which India got its freedom and Pakistan was created laid no such stipulation. Moreover, Sheikh Mohammad Abdullah the leader with the largest following, had personally endorsed the Instrument of Accession. In any case, Mountbatten was, in Oct 1947, only a constitutional head of the Indian Dominion as the Governor General, his opinion and advice was thus not binding on the Government of India. It could well be that taking the precedent of Junagadh, where the Indian Government had overturned the Nawab's decision of acceding to Pakistan by sending in the Army and then holding a plebiscite, Lord Mountbatten felt that the same rule should now apply to Kashmir. Fair enough, although in the case of Kashmir, India had neither overturned the Maharajah's decision to accede to Pakistan, which he had not, nor coerced him into joining India, which Pakistan had, by sending in Pak Army led tribal invaders. In any case Mountbatten was not a referee between India and Pakistan. Even so, the holding of plebiscite was an issue to be settled between the Government of India and the people of Kashmir without any third party coming into the matter, least of all Pakistan. After initial reservations Sardar Patel, then in-charge of the States Ministry had by Nov 1948 started taking greater interest in Kashmir, which after all was his charter. Mr. Nehru, however, inducted Sir Gopalaswami Ayyangar in the Sardar's Ministry to look after Kashmir affairs on his behalf. The Sardar was furious and after an acrimonious correspondence the Sardar offered to resign. (1) It was obvious that Mr. Nehru was under the spell of Mountbatten but in this case he rushed off to seek the backing of Gandhiji. It is now clear from published documents that Mr. Nehru had the habit of running to Mahatma Gandhi and Lord Mountbatten in order to counter the more pragmatic views of his deputy, the Great Sardar. As a result of this psychological handicap he gave in to pressure by Mountbatten to take the Kashmir issue to the United Nations. Earlier, Pakistan had toyed with the idea of raising the issue of Kashmir's accession to India in the UN but Mr. Jinnah was strongly advised against it by the British, since legally Pakistan had no case, for the reasons already stated On the other hand, if India could be prevailed upon to lodge a complaint in the UN as an aggrieved party the Kashmir Question could be manipulated to Pakistan's benefit. This is exactly what the British, through Mountbatten, set about to ensure.

From various documents now becoming public it is clear that Nehru was given a few brain washing sessions and thrown a bait on the lines that since Sheikh Abdullah's influence did not extend outside the Valley it would be politically imprudent to get control of areas with non-Kashmiri, pro-Pakistan populations. A division of Jammu and Kashmir allowing India to retain the Valley and non muslim majority areas of the Jammu province, while giving up the rest to Pakistan could be organised in case India was to refer the matter to the United Nations. Britain would see that such a proposal was adopted. According to Maj Maroof Raza's statement in his book, "War and Peace over Kashmir", Mr. Gopalaswamy Ayyanagar, the leader of the Indian delegation was directed to follow the British delegate's line in the Security Council's debate. The British were to completely renege on what-ever arrangement they may have privately made with Mr. Nehru, who was soon to realise that he had been hugely tricked, with his eyes open by the British. What is more Mr. Nehru had gone ahead and internationalised an issue, which was strictly between India and the people of Kashmir.

By Mar-Apr 48, he now accepted the Army's plans for re-organisation of their forces and a new offensive in J and K. This completely upset the British plans for Pakistan, so the British C-in-C of the Pakistan Army wrote to the Pakistani PM that "it is imperative that the Indian Army is not allowed to advance beyond the general line Uri-Poonch - Naushera". (2) Consequently, major Pakistani formations, which had by now organised themselves after the partition of the British Indian Army, moved into the battle areas. Mr. Nehru continued to twiddle his thumbs. Steadily but surely the Army and the Air Force started pushing the Pakistanis back all along the battle-front, while in the Security Council Mr. Nehru's hand-picked delegation was squeezed out of every position they took in the debate, by the Pakistani delegate Sir Zafar Ullah Khan who was fully supported by the British and on their advice by the Americans as well.

The successes of the Indian Army and Airforce became unserving for Pakistani-British combine. Britain once again got hold of Mr. Nehru's ears. This is now known from some records of the erstwhile India Office, which were declassified a few years back. From these it is clear that the British High Commissioner in Delhi was constantly feeding details of Indian Army's strengths and locations, right upto the battalion levels to his counterpart in Pakistan. Moreover, there appeared to be a gentleman's agreement between the British C-in-C of the Royal Pakistan Airforce and the British C-in-C of the Royal Indian Airforce regarding how far and where the Royal Indian Airforce could/would be used. Even as late as 05 Nov 1948, Message Number 1348 resought the implementation of this agreement. (3). That the British attempts to brain-wash Mr. Nehru met with success is apparent from a perusal of a report dated 22 Nov 1948 by the United Kingdom's High Commissioner in India to his superiors in London. This was at a time when the Indians had achieved remarkable success in re-opening the Zoji La-Leh axis, and in removing the enemy from Dras and Kargil. Indian tanks, used for the first time in the history of Warfare at these heights, were moving around Matyan and Dras; Poonch had been linked-up with and the Pakistan Army was on the run all over. The morale of that country was at its very low, but this is what the British High Commissioner was telling Mr. Nehru (4).

"He (Nehru) gave me an opportunity to give my views on the Kashmir situation which I did as follows- Pakistan's forces on the whole are far better placed than Indian forces because their communications were short, ample and not vulnerable. It followed therefore that there is no military solution to the Kashmir problem; only a political one. He was very thoughtful, trifle gloomy, but did not dispute anything I said; indeed by his gaze and comments gave the impression that he agreed".

The British High Commissioner then makes the startling observation, "there is one other relevant point which I did not mention to Nehru and which I do not intend to raise with him but which I am arranging to feed into him from other and more-professional sources. It is this: there are signs that the morale of troops of the Indian Army is beginning to appear thin. First flush of enthusiasm had subsided, the troops have been fighting a long time, including one winter, and the prospect of another winter does not appeal to them very much; due to very rapid promotions in the Indian Army and in particular Commanding Officers of infantry battalions and equivalent units the leadership is lacking and it is probable that as the winter continues, the spirits of the troop will tend to become more depressed. I hope by making these various representations to Nehru, it will be possible to bring home to him that there is no military solution to this problem and the sooner he turns his mind to some political compromise, the better"

The truth, as has been stated earlier was quite the reverse. The morale of the Indian troops was never higher than at that time after their magnificent victories at Zoji La, Kargil, Poonch, Naushera, Mehndar, Tithwal, and Gurez, Kanzalwan and other places. On the contrary the Pakistan's were down and out. The British were worried that after the winter if the Indians continued to fight, Pakistan would lose most of J and K State including Baltistan and Gilgit. So they concentrated their efforts on the weakest link on the Indian side, the Indian Prime Minister himself. Mr. Nehru finally gave in to their pressure and accepted the UN supervised cease-fire on first Jan 1949. In fact, it would be wrong to fault the British, Mr. Nehru allowed himself to be so done in, a matter he was to regret very much but without learning any lessons from it.

It did not take long for the enormity of his folly to dawn upon Mr. Nehru. He had, among other things let the large strategic landmass of Baltistan, with, its access to Gilgit, the Karakorams including the world's second highest peak K-2 and that ultimate challenge to mountaineers, Nanga Parbat and the world's most glaciated regions outside the Artic Circle to slip out of Indian hands by what can only be termed as his ignorance of military matters and political acumen. Even though he claimed to be an authority on political matters; a claim still staked by his party and family. He tried to somehow retrieve matters by writing to the UN Commission on India and Pakistan, that the Indian Army should move to Baltistan since the area was devoid of major populations except for nomads, implying thereby that the Army had for this reason not occupied Baltistan. In reply, he was told that his views would be considered at the time when the redeployment of Indian troops prior to the plebiscite took place. The crime had been committed and out of this crime were to be born apart from Pakistan Occupied Kashmir (POK), the loss of two thousand square kilometers of Indian territory illegitimately given by Pakistan to China, the bringing together of Pakistani and Chinese frontiers near Gilgit, the amalgamation of Gilgit and Baltistan as Northern Areas of Pakistan after detaching them from POK, the Karakoram highway over the Khunzerab pass, the Pakistani cartographic aggression over the Siachin Glacier and the subsequent Siachin conflict which still goes on, the large scale massacre of Ismaili and Shia populations of Gilgit by Sunni fundamentalists from Pakistan, about which the world has been kept in dark, by Indian lethargy and now of course Kargil'99. If only Mr. Nehru had given more time to Sardar Patel and his military commanders, then he did to Mountbatten! That he had been made a complete fool of by the British was well known to Krishna Menon and that was why Mr. Menon reserved his most caustic and harsh comments for the British delegate in the Security Council debates on Kashmir in the mid-fifties. In the meantime Mr. Nehru had got himself to mount the Chinese pony to take him for another ride.

A single infantry brigade consisting of one regular infantry battalion based at Kargil with one company at Batalik guarded the entire stretch of area from Gund, well short of the Zoji La along the length of the cease-fire line with Pakistan and the Sino-Indian border in Ladakh. One battalion of J and K Militia (now a regular regiment called J and K Light Infantry) from Zoji La to Drass and near upto Kargil, while another militia battalion formed out of the Ladakhi volunteers of the 1948 conflict took over from Leh to the China border. This battalion was to be later honoured with the title of Ladakh Scouts and made into a regular battalion of the Indian Army during the Sino-Indian conflict in 1962. There was a narrow road fit for light vehicles only, running from Baltal below Zoji La to Kargil. Beyond that only jeeps used to move upto a point towards Leh. The militia was a para-military force of the Jammu and Kashmir Government officered partly by Indian Army Officers and partly its own cadre. This very flimsy arrangement, extremely thin in troops and based on a very tenuous and vulnerable line of communication was considered to be adequate to look after such an important area. Whether the condition of the land route was considered adequate for the amount of force level across the Zoji La, or whether this force level itself was determined by the nature of the means of its maintenance is not clear. Both could have been improved and upgraded if the threat had been perceived correctly. Being a low priority for Mr. Nehru, the issue was not ever given serious thought which resulted in the Chinese carving a road, unknown to the Indians, from Singkiang to Lhasa, through Aksai Chin, in proclaimed Indian territory of Ladakh. The rest is of course history and needs no repetition except to highlight a few points. When the cease-fire between India and Pakistan took place on first Jan 1949, it left Pakistan in possession of certain features, which dominated not only the Zoji La Kargil road but also a significant height Pt 13620, which over looked the Kargil town, Indian positions and the airstrip at Kargil. When the Sino Indian problem started coming to a boil the road was frenetically upgraded to take heavier traffic to meet the requirements of large number of troops that were concentrated in Ladakh. During the Sino-Indian conflict the Pakistanis could have very effectively interfered with the Indian movement but did not do so under Western pressure.

In 1965, during the Pakistani attack on Kutch, the local brigade commander at Kargil went ahead and threw the Pakistanis out of Pt 13620 and some other heights. This was, as is usual, a part of the tactics of improving ones defence potential and the brigade commander displayed highly commendable initiative. He was rewarded with disapproval from the authorities and told to return back the positions to Pakistan. A short while later when the Pakistanis launched their famous operation Gibraltar into the Valley in Aug 65 the same brigade commander struck again with those very troops and once more captured pt 13620 and other heights from the enemy. In the aftermath of the Tashkent agreement all these gains were once more handed back to the enemy.

In the 1971 war with Pakistan the local commanders in Ladakh including Kargil again displayed initiative of the highest order. At the height of winter they once more went ahead and captured pt 13620 and other dominating features around Kargil. The Eleventh Gorkha Rifles being the heroes of pt 13620 while the indomitable Ladakh Scouts alongwith elements of the Fourth Gorkha Rifles captured Turtuk, Chorbat La and other features, thus securing the Shyok valley. There were no troops to further exploit these gains. Fortunately, the Line of Control (LOC) which was established in J and K after the Shimla Agreement allowed India to retain control of these important points. However, the final acts of the formal cease-fire line now known as the LOC had yet to played out. Both in the alignment of the old cease fire line and the LOC the delineation ended at a point, referred to by its map reference as NJ 9842, from where the line was explained to go Northwards towards the glaciers. As to why a point on the Karakoram ranges, due North of Pt NJ 9482 was not used to show where the former cease-fire line and the new LOC terminated is not understandable. Perhaps in the case of the old cease-fire line the non-availability of reliable and well-surveyed maps would be the explanation. Large areas along India's borders were then shown as blank un-surveyed areas. That was not the case in 1972. One can therefore, be forgiven the conclusion that officers responsible for delineating the LOC, particularly those of the Indian side, were not careful enough to realise that Pakistan would use any and every loophole in its agreements with India to its advantage. That is exactly what happened. After the 1962 Sino-Indian conflict the Chinese declared a unilateral cease-fire which the Indians accepted quietly. The Chinese pulled back in the then NEFA (now Arunachal Pradesh) but did not do so in Ladakh. The Line of Actual Control (LAC) or cease-fire between the Indian and the Chinese troops ended near the Karakoram pass. The Pakistanis cleverly connected grid reference NJ 9842 with the Karakoram pass to the Northeast, on their maps. Thereby they catagraphically claimed the Siachin Glacier. They had maps published in various brochures meant for mountaineering expeditions to the Karakorams. The Indian Army mountaineers were the first to notice this cartographic aggression as also that Pakistan was issuing permits for climbing peaks which were not in its jurisdiction. Col. N. Kumar, the famous mountaineer who carried out an expedition to the Siachin area highlighted the implications of the Pakistani map aggression and the Indian Army reacted quickly, occupying unbelievable heights in a swift operation. That is how the Siachin battleground was born. The new LOC still allowed a stretch of approximately 60 Kms of the Zoji La-Leh highway to be interfered with by the Pakistani artillery deployed on their side of the LOC. A new alignment further east out of Pak artillery's range would have meant road construction through very difficult terrain, but the result would have been worth the effort. An alternative route through Manali over the Rohtang pass in Himachal Pradesh was subsequently constructed. All this was however well in the future as were the many subsequent events narrated above. Suffice to say that with the UN sponsored and supervised cease fire of Jan 1949, the stage had been set for the many tragedies that were to befall Jammu and Kashmir, including the latest one of Kargil' 99.

PART –II -ALIENATING THE KASHMIRIS

"Jawaharlal Royega" (Jawaharlal Will weep)- Sardar Patel

The next act of naiveté over Kashmir was to be played out in three scenes. Scene one was the special status accorded to Jammu and Kashmir under Article 370 of the Indian constitution. Sheikh Abdullah bamboozled Mr. Nehru into doing so, again against the advice of Sardar Patel. The result was that not only did the people of Kashmir considered themselves to be different from the rest of India, but what was more unfortunate for them was that they were denied the advantages and protections offered to them by the Indian constitution. One of them being free and fair elections under an independent election commission. All elections to the J & K Assembly were rigged. The people of Kashmir were left to the mercies of a few families who enriched themselves from the liberal funds the Central Government made available for the economic development. The Sheikhs growing intransigence led to his dismissal from the Prime Ministership of the State and his arrest. During his long imprisonment, Kashmir was governed by some of the most corrupt and incompetent persons with no popular backing. During Mr. Sadiq's time the National Conference, the party which the Sheikh had founded, converted itself into the Indian National congress with which it merged. It was at this time, circa 1964-65 that a unique event took place of which very few people are aware. A large number of Bihari Muslims assisted by mullahs from Deoband in Uttar Pradesh entered the Valley and settled down, many in the interior of Srinagar. Calling themselves Allah Wales, they married local women and opened Madrassas, which preached

Wahabi Sunni brand of Islam, and complete anti Indian view points. The political leaders- Congress was in power then - made no attempt to stop them, even though by their very act of settling down in the Valley and buying property for madrassas was violative of the State Subject Act. It was not as if the Sate Government was unaware of what was happening, on the contrary it did not want to get embroiled at a political level in a controversy with the Muslim fundamentalist wave that had now entered the Valley. Moreover, the local administration was unable and infact sympathetic to this undercurrent.

Whatever, the Sheikh's reservations may have been about Indo-Kashmir relations, two things must be said to his credit. He was a devout Muslim and a committed Kashmiri. One may say that he was a Kashmiri Muslim nationalist and an inspired opponent of mullah dominated narrow fundamentalist interpretation of Islamic thought. The Congress led governments in Kashmir, in the tradition of that party cutting the nose to spite the face, went along with the undermining of the Kashmiri outlook on Islam, in the hope that thereby the influence of the Sheikh would consequently diminish. After the elevation of Syed Mir Qasim as the Chief Minister the Jamat Islami was encouraged by the Congress to further reduce the Sheikhs influence. (5) This was to have a terrible impact on Kashmiri politics and the Kashmiri Muslim psyche. The first scene of the act to alienate the Kashmiris had now been completed. Immeasurable damage to the Kashmiri social fabric with the open denouncement of Sufisim (so dear to both Kashmiri Muslims and Hindus) had now taken place. Accession to India was questioned. Since Mr. Nehru's time while every effort should have been made to bring

Kashmir closer to the Indian mainstream, in actual terms deep divisions had taken place between people of the Valley and rest of India. The people were encouraged to pressurise the Central Government to spend untold amounts to keep the Kashmiris quiet. Hence, over the last fifty years continuous misrule has only reinforced the Kashmiris' sense of isolation. A railway line would have increased greater mobility of the Kashmiri youth with rest of India, employment and enhanced stronger economic bonds which no religious or similar fundamentalist movements.

The second scene of this act of alienation started with the defeat of Pakistan in the 1971 war. Mrs. Gandhi in an act of excellent statesmanship restored the Shiekh to power. She erred in placing unwarranted faith in Mr. Bhutto to convert the LOC into an international border and similarly she got the wrong impression that the Sheikh would wind-up his party, the Plebiscite Front and joins the Congress. It will be recalled that his original National Conference had been merged with the Congress during his years in the wilderness. This was like expecting him to commit political hara-kiri. He revived his National Conference, parted company with some of his prominent supporters of the Plebiscite Front and went ahead to win an election during the Janata Party regime after the emergency. It was perhaps the high noon of peace in Kashmir never to return again? A number of the Sheikh's opponents joined the Janata Party, the Congress became the main opposition, and Pakistan became irrelevant. The threat of fundamentalist Islam in Kashmir through the Madrassas and the rise of the Jamait horrified the Sheikh. So much so that he decreed a holy war against them, something only a man of his status could do. His efforts soon started bearing success. When Bhutto was hanged in Pakistan the general public in the Valley went for the throat of the Jamait's followers and leaders.

At the same time the Sheikh had to re-establish himself with the Kashmiri Muslims by showing that he had not sold out to the government in Delhi. They were assured that they would be as autonomous as they apparently were when he was first arrested in 1953 and their interests were uppermost in his mind, even if at the expense of Kashmiri Pandits and Jammu Dogras. Consequently he resumed adopting a confrontationist attitude towards the Central government. He also started encouraging Kashmiri Muslims to settle in the upper areas of Doda and in Ladakh, while Gujjar Muslims were planned to be settled in Jammu. The idea was to create a constituency of his own in areas where his influence was weak. He had learnt his lesson from his previous political experience of being unable to gain popularity outside the Valley.

The Shimla Agreement signed by Mrs. Gandhi with Mr. Bhutto made a major gain for Pakistan. Kashmir was recognised as an area of dispute between India and Pakistan. Para 6 of the agreement noted; " Both Governments agree that their respective Heads will meet again at a mutually convenient time in the future and that in the meanwhile, the representatives of the two sides will meet to discuss further modalities and arrangements for the establishment of durable peace and normalisation of relations, including the question for repatriation of prisoners of war and civilian internees, **a final settlement of Jammu and Kashmir** and the resumption of diplomatic relations"(Emphasis authors').

This country has been led to believe that the Shimla Agreement took place consequent to an "un-written", understanding between the Indian Prime Minister Mrs. Gandhi and her Pakistani counterpart Mr. Bhutto that in due course the LOC would be converted into an international border. Pakistan of course denies all that now, as it may well do in future. Private arrangements are not public guarantees. What is a public guaranty is the fact that Kashmir got recognised as a dispute between Pakistan and India and it was to be settled along with the return of prisoners of war, etc and resumption of diplomatic ties. In the event, the last two events took place without any insistence by India concurrently to have the seal of legal approval stamped on the private Gandhi-Bhutto understanding on Kashmir. Mr. Bhutto however went ahead to implement that part of his private bargain with Mrs. Gandhi which was advantageous to Pakistan. He promptly detached Baltistan and Gilgit from Pakistan Occupied Jammu and Kashmir (PoK) and amalgamated them with mainland Pakistan. The Mirs of Hunza and Gilgit etc were unceremoniously kicked out. India did not even raise a bleat because Mr. Bhutto was, in manner of speaking only acting within the understanding with Mrs. Gandhi. No alarm bells rang in Delhi as to why Pakistan did not absorb the complete PoK and thus automatically make the LOC an international border with India. It should have been obvious that the northern areas had been taken over by Pakistan from the jurisdiction of any future Indo-Pak settlement of Kashmir. And even if alarm bells did ring, Indira Gandhi was now fighting for her political survival once the euphoria of the '71 war was over. One of the battles, which Mrs. Gandhi launched, was once again against the Abdullah family. By now the Sheikh was a very sick man. Soon, he appointed his son as the political successor and Mrs. Gandhi helped him in the fond belief that the son would be more amenable, than the father was, in bringing Kashmir into the mainstream of Indian polity and himself into the Congress.

When the Shiekh passed away the genuine honour given to him by the rest of India, as well as the smooth succession of Farooq Abdullah to his father's power, created an unprecedented pro-Indian wave in the Valley. In due course however Mr. Bhutto was to be hanged and Martial Law declared in Pakistan. The Soviet Union had invaded Afghanistan and soon Punjab was to surface as a major secessionist problem, after the return of Mrs. Gandhi to power. All the plus points regarding Kashmir were squandered by Mrs. Gandhi, who looked upon any opposition to herself as traitorous to the Country. In the process of strengthening his hold on the Valley Muslims, Farooq had willy-nilly to play his father's role, pro-Delhi on the Jammu side of the Banihal pass and anti-Delhi on the Srinagar side. The platform he chose to do so was that of anti Congress (read Mrs. Gandhi) political parties in the rest of the Country. The Kashmiris applauded him. The states person in Mrs. Gandhi would have welcomed this indirect entry of the Valley Muslims into mainstream Indian polity even if in opposition to her. Farooq who in any case was giving a poor administration to the state was pulled and buffeted, with his family members being pitted against him. Mrs. Gandhi's hatchet men were two people who were to later join the BJP, one of them only recently. Farooq was thrown out by his brother-in-law Mr. G.M. Shah, who himself was installed as the Chief Minister. He and his cronies had a field day; the Madrassas were back in business and the pro-Pakistan lobby back into its own. Boys who had joined the Madrassas in the sixties, now young men had started trekking across the mountain ranges to go to PoK to get training in arms, some even to join the struggle in Afghanistan.

Warnings by the Army and other intelligence agencies that trouble was a brewing were ignored. By the time Farooq was reinstalled by Rajiv Gandhi much damage had been done. Even then there was a last chance to put things right. In the elections to the State assembly Farooq should have been allowed to fight the elections on his own. He would have won with a slight majority, anti-Farooq but not anti-India forces would have joined up with the Congress. Thus the strength or weakness of the fundamentalist pro-Pakistan elements would have been shown up. Even if these elements had won the elections, which was highly unlikely, they had to operate within the four walls of the State's and Indian Constitutions. Anything of serious damage to India emanating from them would have called for their immediate ouster legally. Chances are that a few of them would have elected and no more. That was not to because of the Congressmen who unable to think beyond their own interest and more importantly unable to remain out of power foisted themselves on the unfortunate Farooq Abdullah. The latter in turn, in a fit of unnecessary caution allowed elections to be rigged. The disgust of people was complete. The last nail in the coffin of the then Indian standing in the Valley had been driven. Pakistan was soon to provide the pallbearers.

The third scene in the act of alienation was the insurgency in Kashmir. There was gross intelligence failure, a very ham-handed counter-insurgency effort with senior commanders both in Udhampur and Srinagar, and ofcourse not to speak of Delhi which was completely lost. Indian attention was also divided towards Sri Lanka. The implications of Pakistani successes in Afghanistan were talked about but never taken into account in military planning vis-à-vis Kashmir. As early as 1990, a suggestion was made that the task of fighting the insurgency in Kashmir and guarding the LOC should be bifurcated. This was not accepted, more for personal rather than tactical reasons. This and much more that should have happened earlier is now being done post-Kargil 99. The change of personalities at the Corps and Command Headquarters levels in Srinagar and Udhampur from 95-96 onward brought about a sea change in the approach to counter-insurgency operations. There was a very visible diminishing of insurgency in the Valley. The local insurgent cadres either surrendered, or were eliminated or came over ground to become counter-insurgents themselves. The control of insurgent violence passed into the hands of foreign mercenaries and alumni of Pakistani Madrassas, Afghan veterans and such like elements, all controlled by the omnipotent ISI. An elected government took over power in Jammu and Kashmir and things on the face of it appeared to be on the mend. "On the face of it".

PART III - DURING KARGIL 99

The Pakistani Misadventure

Kashmir has been a pathological obsession with Pakistan. On the other hand Indian efforts to cure Pakistan of this obsession have been pathetic. Pakistan puts forward a number of arguments for possessing Kashmir. Being a Muslim majority state, it should have gone to Pakistan at the time of partition. Rubbish, the princely states had to go the dominion where their rulers led them. That was the stipulation, a stipulation fully supported by Mr. Jinnah himself. Kashmir was strategically important for Pakistan. The British threw this idea into the Pakistani arguments. They felt that if Indian borders were to touch those portions of Pakistan which in any case were brought into Pakistan by fraud i.e., the North West Frontier Province India would undo Pakistan's existence. Consider the appreciation of the British Commander-in-Chief of the Pakistan Army, General Sir Douglas Gracey given to his Government in 1948: -

"If Pakistan is not to face another problem of about 2,750,000 uprooted from their homes; if India is not allowed to sit on the doorsteps of Pakistan to the rear and on the flank, at liberty to enter at her will and pleasure; if civilian and military morale is not to be affected to a dangerous extent; and if subversive political forces are not to be let loose within Pakistan itself, it is imperative that the Indian Army is not allowed to advance beyond the general time Uri-Poonch-Naushera". (The underlined portion by the author. Last sentence already quoted earlier' (4)".

Another argument advanced is that since the waters of three rivers of Pakistan, i.e. Indus, Jhelum, Chenab and their tributaries originate or come through Kashmir the territory must belong to Pakistan. A most ludicrous argument if their was one. Nepal should, according this reasoning become a part of India; India of Bangladesh and so on. In any case the Indus waters treaty has been most advantageous to Pakistan while tying the hands of Kashmiris.

At this stage it must be emphasized and re-emphasized most strongly that Pakistan from the day it came into existence till now, never possessed even an inch of Kashmir. The old Jammu and Kashmir State as it existed before partition consisted of Jammu, Kashmir, Ladakh, Baltistan and Gilgit. It was a composite state generally known as Kashmir. At present India holds the entire Kashmir Valley which is the actual Kashmir parts of Jammu small portions of old Baltistan (Kargil etc) and Ladakh. What Pakistan holds and calls Azad Kashmir (PoK) are non-Kashmiri areas, inhabited by people ethnically, linguistically and culturally different from the Kashmiris. Therefore even by right of possession, Pakistan has no right on the Kashmir Valley. Next, with Pakistan having divided itself into a sovereign Bangladesh and the rump Pakistan that exists even the Muslim card is not its ace. India, after Indonesia has the second largest Muslim population. Finally, Pakistan itself failed to implement the Security Council resolutions which mandated that Pakistan withdraw its troops from Jammu and Kashmir, the local administration of the State be restored, Indian troops be re-deployed and only then a plebiscite be held. The clock cannot be turned back to please Pakistan. That is exactly what Pakistan has been trying to do all these years.

Pakistan's military strategy over Kashmir is based on three parameters. Firstly, a sponsored or spontaneous uprising in the Muslim areas of Indian held Jammu and Kashmir, particularly the Valley. Secondly, the creation of a corridor between the PoK and the Valley by securing a passage through the high mountain ranges surrounding the Valley and held by the Indian Army. This would allow for unrestricted flow of weapons, including heavier ones into "liberated" areas secured by local (?), mercenary elements already in the Valley. Simultaneously isolate the Valley by interdicting the road link between Jammu and the Valley. Thirdly, to get the matter so internationalised that India would be forced to accept a settlement of Kashmir issue if not completely on Pakistan's terms, at least on those highly favourable to it. There was one problem that Pakistan found daunting, in so far as a military confrontation was concerned. The rules of war between India and Pakistan as they appeared to have been laid down in the '47-48' conflict in Kashmir were that military operations would be restricted to Jammu and Kashmir alone. India had accepted this informal arrangement as is obvious since no action was taken against any other part of Pakistan in retaliation for Pakistani troops entering Kashmir. In '65 India changed the rules and Pakistan's plans came unstuck. In order to offset the Indian superiority in conventional forces Pakistan opted for the nuclear route. The '71 war between India and Pakistan was not over Kashmir but on the question of Bangladesh. Kashmir for once was incidental. In 1990 when major insurgent groups crossed over from PoK into the Valley, India could/should have crossed the LOC to destroy concentrations and training camps in PoK. India did not do so. Incidentally, many Indian military commentators who had recently been shouting over the media demanding that the LOC be crossed when Pakistan invaded Kargil were then in very high positions in the Army. None of them appears to have thumped the table at that time, demanding that the LOC be crossed. Pakistan was so confident that India would not dare do so that in fact it went ahead with its exercise, Zarb-e-Momin, the biggest exercise held till then by the Pakistan Army. This exercise took place by diverting major Pakistani formations away from the Indo-Pak border—such was the Pakistani confidence. This was undoubtedly the result of cowardly Pakistani threats of a nuclear reaction to any move by India to launch operations either outside Kashmir or even across the LOC. Whatever the Pakistani threat it was enough to cool down the military ardour if any of various Indian decision makers.

At this stage it will be appropriate to consider the terms under which Pakistan would agree to a solution of Kashmir. These have been gleaned as well as hypothesized from the records of various discussions held between India and Pakistan in the past; particularly after the 1962 Sino-Indian conflict, statements of Pakistani leaders from time to time and views expressed by their leaders and opinion makers in public or private. They are given in the order of priority as follows: -

(a) Apart from the Hindu majority areas of Jammu region and the Buddhist majority areas of Ladakh, the rest of Jammu and Kashmir goes to Pakistan.

(b) A plebiscite in the Valley as well as in the muslim majority areas of Jammu and PoK (Azad Kashmir) to determine their future. Ladakh and Northern Areas remain with India and Pakistan respectively.

(c) A division of the Valley between India and Pakistan with area west of lines Qazi-Gund-River Jhelum-Northern part of Wular lake- Northwards to the Line of Control in Gurez-Kanzalwan areas to merge with Pakistan. East of this line with India. No change to the possession of PoK, Northern Areas, Jammu region and Ladakh with the present LOC becoming a permanent border along with the proposed line in the valley.

(d) Lastly, is a proposal recently talked of in some Pakistani papers as emanating from US think tanks and establishment likely to be considered by Pakistan? It suggests that the Northern Areas and Ladakh region remain part of Pakistan and India respectively. PoK

(Azad Kashmir) and Indian Kashmir (perhaps including Jammu) to have maximum autonomy while remaining under Pakistan and India, but with their respective assemblies to be elected under international supervision (read UN) and finally after five years(?) these assemblies to decide on their future affiliation with either Pakistan or India. Their decision is mandatory and binding under international guaranty.

The Shimla Agreement had made one binding commitment on India and Pakistan. In para 4(ii) it states:-

"In Jammu and Kashmir the line of control resulting from the cease-fire of 1971 shall be respected by both the sides without prejudice to the recognized position on either side. Neither side shall seek to alter it unilaterally irrespective of mutual differences and legal interpretations. Both sides further undertake to refrain from the threat or use of force in violation of this line".

Pakistani cartographic aggression of the LOC North of map reference NJ 9842 was its first attempt to meddle with the binding terms of the Shimla Agreement. The Indian response to it was to restore the status quo ante as it existed at the time of the Shimla Agreement.

Having been worsted in the mercenary fuelled insurgency in the Valley, Pakistan decided to put into effect a plan which was probably being nurtured since '91-'92, the time when the Indian Army thinned out from east of Zoji-La to reinforce troops in the Valley. Besides, the Indian nuclear tests and Pakistan's response to it in May '98 raised the specter of a nuclear holocaust in the sub-continent, a specter Pakistan has been trying to conjure up in order to get international support. The rapid Talibization of Pakistan society, availability of Afghan Mercenaries, a perceived state of political instability in India, all these encouraged Pakistan in its adventure. Thus the Pakistani aim was clear and succinct; gain major strategic advantages in J and K in area of its own choosing, raise the fear of a nuclear war in case India reacted anywhere outside the zone of immediate conflict, particularly outside J and K and press for international intervention.

The immediate tactical aims were obviously: -

(a) To block the Srinagar-Leh-Siachin road.

(b) Capture as much area as possible between the LOC from Drass to Batalik and force attrition on Indians, while at the same time declaring it as a liberated territory.

(c) Open-up a route for insurgents to enter into the Valley and Doda by forcing a passage through the main mountain barrier; the great Himalayan range.

The operation must have been planned over quite sometime and at the highest level as one of the military options. For its actual execution regular troops of 2nd, 3rd, 4th and 5th Battalions of the Northern Light Infantry were grouped with Special Service Troops; some Afghan mercenaries; Islamic fundamentalist groups provided by Lashkar-e-Taiba based outside Lahore; Harkat-ul-Mujahadeen who are the former Harkat-ul-Ansar declared a terrorist organisation by the USA; and the Hizb-ul-Mujaheedin the militant arm of Jamait-e-Islami, the founding father of the Taliban Movement. All these were grouped under Pakistani regular formations located in the Northern Areas. The description which follows is based on the Article "Pakistan's Aggression in Kashmir

99" by Maj. Gen. (Retd) Afsir Karim, AVSM, in the July 99 issue of Akrosh-Volume 2, Number 4.

It is evident that three separate forces composed of the elements indicated above were formed as under, starting from west to northeast: -

(a) 82 (PAK) Brigade located at Minimarg for operations in Kargil-Drass Sector.

(b) 62 (PAK) Brigade located at Skardu for operations in Batalik Sector.

(c) 232 (PAK) Brigade located at Darsam for operations aimed at capturing Turtuk.

From other sources it appears that nearly 300 personnel were operating in Mashkoh valley and reached upto four Km into the Indian side of the LOC. Again a similar group reached about 15 Km towards Drass covering Tololing and Tiger Hill aiming to cut the Zoji-La-Leh road. In Kaksar, again a group of 100 was to threaten Kargil. Finally, a group of 350 entered Batalik and threatened Leh-Siachin route—rather difficult by initially capturing three ridgelines.

A brigade less a battalion, that is a force of two battalions and up to 2000 mercenaries was to be kept in reserve. Twenty artillery batteries located on Pakistan side of the LOC provided support. There were a number of engineer detachments, local porters and probably in the initial stages at least helicopters for carrying out either troop movement and/or building up supplies. Use of snowmobiles has also been reported.

Maj. Gen. Afsir Karim also suggests that the Pakistani operation be divided into four phases. These were, to quote him: -

Phase I.

* Designated groups were to occupy unheld areas or those vacated by the Indian Army during winter by stealth in Chorbat-La, Batalik, Drass and Mashkoh valley.

* Interdiction of the Srinagar-Leh road (the national highway NH 1A) between Drass and Kargil by artillery fire and physical occupation wherever possible.

* Attack on Turtuk to facilitate operations in the Shyok valley against logistic bases supplying Siachin.

Phase II

* Highly trained mercenaries supported by Special Services Group elements were to enter Kashmir Valley across the Great Himalayan Range to create disturbances and subvert administration.

* Prepare the ground for the occupation of the Pahalgam-Anantnag belt in the Valley.

Phase III

* 'Liberation' of Sonamarg, Pahalgam and Anantnag districts by irregular forces led by Afghan war veterans and Pakistani Army troops posing as Mujahideen.

Phase IV

* Liberation of the Doda-Kishtwar belt by armed mercenaries.

* Cutting of logistic support routes to Siachin.

Though this author agrees with the possibility of Phases I and II, the other phases are arguably over ambitious being devoid of logistic and artillery support. Also, it has to be remembered by Pakistan that the number of formations India can bring into an area of conflict is too many for Pakistan to manage. Yes, creating a situation where international pressure would mount on India was always a basis for all Pakistani mis-adventures. This was premised on Pakistan's military success and India's inability to take casualties. In the event, the Indian Army after being taken by surprise of its own making responded magnificently. The Indian Air Force did sterling work and the use of the Air Force showed that the Indian Government was prepared to raise the stakes if so required. The recapture of Tololing and Tiger Hill in Drass sector and Jubbar and Kokar Thang in Batalik by the Indian Infantry daringly supported by the Air Force and brilliantly by the Indian Artillery broke the Pakistani soldiers will to fight and they started vacating one position after another. At the same time for once our Ministry of External Affairs moved and moved with determination and finesse so conspicuous by their absence over the last four decades in our diplomatic efforts. Pakistan's misadventure in the Kargil came to an end with ignominious results except in helping them to infiltrate a large bands of trained mercenaries into the Valley through gaps created by the diversion of troops from the Valley to Kargil.

The Indian Response.

If future analyst with the benefit of hindsight and published declassified documents write about the conflict in Kargil, they will unhesitatingly agree about two things; the indomitable courage of the Indian officers and men from the Army and the Air Force and the brilliant diplomatic coup that the Indian External

Affairs Ministry brought about in swinging the world opinion in India's favour on the issue of Kargil. And once the pettiness of current electioneering settles down, it will be accepted by all fair minded people that Kargil was a victory in every manner of which every self-respecting Indian can be proud of. It will also have to be conceded by all, even if by some grudgingly, that the Central Government handled the crises with elan, confidence and courage. Having said all this, some harsh facts have to be recorded in order to draw lessons for the future.

Intelligence.

Much has been said about intelligence failure, as if this is something new. All Indian security efforts have had one thing in common, either poor intelligence or the complete lack of it. For the sake of the layman it would be appropriate to elaborate a little on the subject of intelligence. Intelligence is not mere information. Information or raw information so to say is gathered by various sources; agents, informers, satellite pictures, air-photographs and surveillance; troops in contact; smugglers, electronic eaves dropping and so on. Even seemingly innocuous looking newspaper articles, advertisements, Governmental-shopping sprees, industrial espionage – the list is endless. The more energetic our information gathering organisation the more areas of information it will explore. But, information gathering agencies cannot go about gathering information ad infinitum and create an information over-load which would result in utter chaos. Therefore, information-gathering agencies have to be tasked by being provided specific questions by the users of the information. For this purpose the users themselves must be clear as to what they are looking for. As an example from Kargil, were specific information asked about any unusual troop concentrations, reconnaissance, by the enemy, improvement of communications in his areas, new gun areas or heli-pads being constructed and such like activities which indicate the future intentions of the enemy. This sort of questioning can only take place if there is/was a threat perception from Pakistan in the Kargil sector.

Raw information once gathered by one agency is checked and cross-checked with similar information gathered by other agencies. More than one agency is always tasked for gathering the same information in order to confirm reinforce or reject it. For example – again citing Kargil – Snowshoes were purchased by Pakistan from abroad. For a moment leaving aside the veracity of this information, was any similar matching information like training of large number of troops in high altitude warfare available so that the two could be associated. Once information has been confirmed by cross checking, it is then put together and an assessment made of what is likely to happen. This is 'intelligence' and it must be disseminated to the users at the earliest for them to make use of it in order to counter and pre-empt the opponents action. Intelligence given late is as useless for the recipients.

There are a number of agencies charged with information gathering. The foremost amongst them is the Research and Analysis Wing (RAW) responsible for external intelligence. The Armed Forces have very limited resources. The intelligence activity gets limited to information obtained by troops in contact with the enemy, local air surveillance and local agents. The other organisations have their own priorities; thus the police is after criminals and mafia, the BSF after smugglers, gunrunners and so on. There is always a nexus amongst criminal and anti-national elements more often then not fostered by a hostile power, in this case Pakistan. Each agency rushes off with its own scraps of information up its own channels of command. Often some very important information of use to another agency, in the present case the Armed Forces, particularly the Army either never reaches it or reaches much after any action can be taken. For example an agency claiming that reports regarding possible infiltration into Kargil came to its knowledge in say Aug '98 and then making this information available to the Army in Mar/Apr 99 has been of no use. By then the infiltration had perhaps already taken place. Then again, if one agency informs its higher ups-may be even to the top Government levels but with no similar collaboration from others, then the information will be glossed over. Here too, if those responsible for acting on the information – say in the case of Kargil the Army - either found that in actuality no infiltration had taken place or their own sources were unable to confirm such information. They are either likely to ignore it, or ask further questions (tasking the intelligence agencies) to confirm or completely reject the information.

Lastly, all information converted into intelligence reaches the Joint Intelligence Committee (JIC) to enable it to carry out an overall review, assessments, future threat perceptions and so on. All this has been explained in a very simplistic language, to indicate the processes of intelligence activity. Any thing can go wrong in this chain of: -

* <u>Information gathering</u>; based on questions raised by interested agencies. The latter themselves may pose

faulty questions or none at all. Therefore faulty answers or answers presumed to be of no use to certain agencies may be obtained by information gatherers.

* The Collation and interpretation of the information collected may be faulty. Faulty interpretation normally resulting out of preconceived ideas or appreciation may lead interpreters and analysts to reject information which does not fit into their presumed ideas, even though the information may be correct. Such a possibility could have been taken in the case of Kargil.

* The Dissemination of the intelligence may be slow rendering it out of date. It may not reach the proper user of the intelligence at all. This is often the result of poor coordination amongst intelligence agencies and recipients of their services, i.e. RAW and the Armed Forces, BSF and the Army, Military Intelligence and lower headquarters.

Indian Army's Actions

It has been stated earlier that as far back as 1990 a suggestion was made by this author that the Corps Headquarters in Srinagar should only look after the LOC while the counterinsurgency operations in the valley should be controlled by another Headquarters. The proposal was turned down on the specious argument that since the insurgency was controlled and sustained from across the LOC the same Headquarters should control both actions. One of the reasons given for bifurcating the tasks was the inherent danger that with the same Commander and Headquarters controlling both, there was always the likely-hood of their becoming fully embroiled either with the counter-insurgency operations to the detriment of operations along the LOC or because of an increase of pressure on the LOC having their attention taken away from the counter-insurgency operations in the Valley. The Pakistan consequently always had a double option of either increasing the operations along the LOC to relieve the Indian counter-insurgency pressure on their proxy warriors in the Valley or increase the efforts of the proxy warriors in order to force a diversion of Indian troops manning the LOC. It was also suggested that as a part of Pakistani plans it could be expected on their part to open up a corridor into the Valley, possibly in or around the Kupwara sector.

An ineffective Northern Command Headquarters, an obstinate Srinagar Corps Headquarters and a rather befuddled Army Headquarters summarily dismissed all the above ideas. The latter as has been stated earlier because their attention was by and large riveted on Sri Lanka. Kashmir was therefore left to be handled by the local commanders. The period when these ideas were mooted was 1991-92. The pressure of Sri Lanka was on; we had still to come to grips with the insurgency in Kashmir; the Valley was in turmoil; Sopore had been declared a 'Liberated' area by the insurgents and no military movement could take place through it; since the presumed civilian bloodshed that would take place in cleaning the town was unacceptable to commanders at Srinagar and Udhampur. The Headquarters in Udhampur were still looking on their task as an "aid to civil power". The pressure of infiltration in, around Kupwara, and East of it through areas known as the Northern gullies had been mounting. Consequently the Headquarters in Srinagar did exactly as had been predicted. It pulled out large concentrations of troops from East of Zoji La area, i.e. troops responsible for Kargil – Drass – Batalik sectors. Even the formation looking after the Chinese side was milked. The temptation for the Pakistanis to try their luck in Kargil was thus created seven to eight years back.

Perhaps one of the beliefs which allowed this thinning down of troops from Kargil sector was the difficult terrain in the area and a comparative lack of any insurgent activity in Ladakh – Zoji La sector, except the odd shelling and futile attempts to capture this or that post in Siachin. Our planners keep on forgetting an excellent dictum of late General K Sundarji. Said in the context of warfare in the desert he observed that one of the greatest means available to an attacker for achieving surprise is to operate over terrain considered to be impassable by the defender. This can be done by superior technological means, in the form of high class and speedy engineer and logistic support, specialized troops and equipment.

One can understand the immediate necessity of pulling out troops from East of Zoji-La to reinforce the LOC in the Valley but in due course the gaps created should have been filled up. This was not done possibly due to an absence of foresight, which demanded of the Indians actions resulting in: -

* Not providing the opponent any window of opportunity to wage an armed conflict.

* Having force levels that would ensure a defeat or such a costly victory for the opponent that he would avoid conflict.

* Continuous thinking of the opponents next course of action.

Keeping all these points in mind it is rather strange that with Pakistan having met with a reasonable set back in its proxy war in the Valley, the Indians left a window of opportunity open to be exploited by Pakistan in Kargil. Blaming this or that agency for what was clearly a failure of military prudence, foresight and consequent anticipatory planning is therefore unfair. The increase in the volume of shelling by Pakistan should have alerted all the Commanders of the chain that Pakistan was preparing something sinister. As for the Commanders at lower levels specially the local brigade Commander; the less said about actions the better. Had they done as much running around and shown as much diligence as they are in handing out classified letters, cultivating political patrons, things may well have been different.

Finally, to conclude this part of the discussion it has to be re-emphasised that the manner in which the operations at the divisional and lower levels were conducted once battle was joined, the innovative use of the artillery and the well handled air operations were an example of good training, courage and leadership which can never be over-praised.

The Foreign Support to India's Course

The Government acted brilliantly in handling the Kargil crises and thereby garnering international support for India's cause. All this of-course was predicated on Indian military success. After the initial setback the Indian Army and the Air Force left no one in doubt that the Pakistanis would be thrown out, dead or alive. Even the American spokesmen had no hesitancy in saying that either the Pakistanis would have to withdraw or will be thrown out. The world also noticed that India observed extreme restraint in not only avoiding retaliating against Pakistan in an area of India's choosing but also even in crossing the LOC. India had to take comparatively higher casualties in doing so and a highly disciplined Army and Air Force accepted the constraint laid down by the Civilian Political Government. Unlike Pakistan where the debate as to whether the Government was even fully kept informed by an almost autonomous Army and the ISI Continues. Moreover, the growing "Talibization" of Pakistan is a cause of worry all round including for China and Russia. And finally the possession of nuclear weapons and missiles by Pakistan has taken away its image of being a poor helpless country being constantly bullied by an unprincipled over bearing bully of an India. Pakistan is now hoist by its own nuclear petard.

Beyond Kargil '99

Mrs. Thatcher was once reported to have said that a true leader converts a crisis into an opportunity. The Kargil crisis offers an opportunity for India to once and for all, lay down the final solution to the Kashmir problem. What this solution is will have to be worked out by consensus by all the political parties in the new Parliament. Some possible solutions Pakistan has in mind have been discussed earlier. Which one of these India is prepared to accept? Perhaps, India can at the best accept the present LOC as an international border and no more. Conditions in terms of military capabilities, surmounting the insurgency in Kashmir and bringing the valley closer to main land India will have to be created to make it difficult for Pakistan to think of any other option to get a better deal than this. Certainly military options for that country should become so unproductive that they are given up in so far as dealing with India, including over Kashmir, is concerned. That way the malevolent influence of Pakistan's Army over that country's political affairs will also be considerably reduced, much to the benefit of the people of Pakistan.

The "Talibization" of Pakistan is a danger that effects Pakistan and the region at large including India. The Indian political effort, must create a situation where-in a Muslim feels more and more secure, free, capable of realizing his or her potential and in every way equal to any other Indian. In fact, Muslims of Pakistan should point to India, as a haven for true Islam, not infected by fundamentalist mullahs, illiterate opinion makers and feudal leaders. This duty to India revolves on organizations like the VHP and the RSS amongst others, who, to use Mr. M.D. Nalpats words in the Times of India; must prevent the "Wahabisation of the Hindu society". Why only for Muslims, for each and every Indian, irrespective of his or her cast, creed, colour, social moorings and language, let India be that great Banyan tree whose roots were nurtured by the martyrs of Kargil. A tree giving shade to all without asking questions.

The findings and the recommendations of the Subramanyam Committee must be discussed dispassionately and implemented honestly. And finally let this be the first and last time that petty politics drags the Armed Forces into dirty politics.

References

1.Arun Shourie ; " A Secular Agenda". P-150: ASA Publications, A 31 West End, New Delhi – 110 021 – 1994.

2.Maj. Gen. Fazal Muqeem Khan – The Story of The Pakistan Army – Oxford University Press – 1963.

3.Dr. Sudhir S Bloeria – The Battles of Zoji-La – 1948 Har Anand Publications Pvt Ltd New Delhi – 1997.

4.Ibid.

5.Maroof Raza, Maj. Akrosh – Jul 99, P-36.

Connected reading by the author

1.Jammu and Kashmir Operations. 1947-48, The Other Version: USI Journal Jul-Sep 92.

2.An Agenda for Kashmir : Indian Defence Review Oct-Dec 94

3.Kashmir: The Way Forward: Indian Defence Review Oct-Dec 95.

4

Kargil Perspective

Major General Y. Bahl (Retd.)

Since the early 1950's the under developed and developing countries of the South Asian Region have remained embroiled in armed conflicts which if not checked may graduate from the use of conventional weapons to the exploitation of nuclear devices. In fact, today South Asian Region has come to be known as a volatile area of the world. This impression has probably been derived from the perpetual instability that is perceived in the region of India and Pakistan – an instability which has firmly become part of their economic and political under development as well as their everlasting rivalry. It is widely recognised that deterrence breakdown between India and Pakistan may lead to use of nuclear weapons, which would have serious repercussions and may provoke Sino-Indian competition to a dangerous level. It may also encourage other South Asian countries to persue nuclear weapons programme. However, as both the countries have very limited nuclear arsenal, and its use may draw adverse opinion of super power, it would remain as deterrence compelling the two nation to restrict their revelry to the usage of conventional weaponry. Further, for the first time India is poised to secure great power capabilities, thereby promising to make Pakistan irrelevant as a long term competitor. Infact, the Sino – Indian rivalry may tend to become the dominant feature of South Asian geopolitics in the new millennium. Therefore, it is an imperative for India, to concentrate in a direction, which would bring stability in South Asia and avoid getting embroiled in arms conflict with Pakistan.

Today both India and Pakistan are probably the most dissatisfied states since the partition of 'Akhand Bharat' (United India) in 1947. The two nations witnessed this traumatic event, creation of a nation through mass migration and death of more than half a million people in violence which accompanied the migration — an unparalleled event of the world history. While India considered partition as unnecessary but complete, Pakistan accepted it as inevitable but fundamentally incomplete because of Kashmir – predominantly a Muslim state which remained in India. Efforts to annex Kashmir, are emotionally essential for Pakistan, as it was the last component essential to complete the vision of her 'Baba E Kaum' Mr. Mohhammed Ali Jinah who desired for a Cohesive Republic composed of all the adjoining Muslim Majority areas. However, with the passage of time, other priorities and strategic requirements have over taken this emotional ethos. Today her constant worry is the longevity and survival of the source of her agricultural and economic wealth – "the water" which flows into Pakistan through Jammu and Kashmir and Kargil of Ladakh. Indus, Jhelum and Chenab rivers either originate in J&K or flow through it into Pakistan. The "India Water Treaty" of 1960 obligation assures the constant supply of this water to Pakistan with a rider or precondition that India will have a preference over it for her domestic requirement of Jammu and Kashmir and Ladakh. Therefore, any effort by India to harness its flow is bound to be viewed with suspicion. The other causes of Pakistan's current attitude are – fear about India to undo Pakistan – her lack of geographical depth together with easterly locations of her industries, vital installations and important communication centers. Further with the geographical location of Jammu and Kashmir, Pakistan feels she has been outflanked and her all vital installations are within striking distance from two different directions. Therefore, the instability in relationship has episodically surfaced in acute form. Both the nations have fought three major wars since the independence in 1947 and both came close to war in early 87,90 and now in 99. Pakistan is not confident of securing her objectives through war because of military superiority of India and declining help from her friends in the past. Hence, Pakistan's involvement in launching a proxy war against India has to be viewed in the context of exploiting weakness in counter balancing India's superiority. This would continue with or without Kashmir and irrespective of nature of Government in Pakistan.

The Indian continent is invariably viewed, as a flash point in global politics where deterrence break down, may lead to nuclear use, which is most unlikely. There is no over assessment in stating that this continent is likely to enjoy an extended period of 'deformed stability' that will last for at least another decade. This peculiar form of stability may be attributed to the inability of Pakistan to attain political objectives through war. Therefore, it will be appropriate to assume that well planned and premedicated conventional war may remain absent for some time to come, though Pakistan, as mentioned earlier, will continue with sub-conventional violence waged with different levels of intensity. It is unlikely to see Pakistan and India prosecuting conventional war of unlimited aims, in the foreseeable future. It should be accepted that Pakistan's military capabilities are simply imaginary to support the pursuit of an unlimited war with India, while India by contrast appears to possess formidable military capabilities – but these are insufficient to overwhelm Pakistan within the constraints of a short war. Why did Pakistan army endanger the peace and prosperity of her nation by intruding into Kargil sector in May 99? Was the strength and effort applied considered adequate to isolate Ladakh and force India to release pressure applied on Bolafond Glacier in Siachen? Pakistan's endeavour to intrude deep into Drass and Batalik area of Kargil Sector successfully without firing a single shot should not be attributed to their military prowess but due to the complacence of Indian military commanders at all levels. Also, for having divorced the laid down standard operating procedures warranting maintenance of surveillance and constant vigil over the porous line of control. Number of casualties both in terms of men and equipment suffered by the Indian Army in evicting the Pakistani troops entrenched in rocky and rugged high altitude mountainous terrain was expected to be much higher then actually suffered as mountains always help the defender more than the attacker. This time it was the infamous ISI of Pakistan, who having failed to execute OP-TOPAC, successfully tried to hide her imbecility, managed to convince the military commanders and lure the government of anticipated rich dividends for undertaking such operations across the line of control. Since it was considered to be most cost effective approach to grab vital areas of Indian territory, the military commander fell for it without realising the long-term consequence. On the other hand, it is also possible that military commanders may have compromised with the ISI, as both disliked the enunciation of the policy 'Bullock Cart to Bus Ride' by the two nations. Mr. Nawaz Shrief as a Prime Minister should have known about the developments on Kargil border but one may accept his ignorance as far as it relates to the degree and extent in execution of the 'Intrusion plans for Kargil' (Ref.tele conversation between PM India and Pakistan of May 99). The absence of three service chiefs during the reception hosted by Mr. Nawaz Sharief to welcome the Indian Prime Minister on arrival in Pakistan by Bus; reinforces these views further. Can service chiefs afford to act indifferently to the government policy unless they are as powerful as the government of the state or they have the concurrence of the head of the state to do so. In Mr. Sultan Shahin's words on Farcial Pak Democracy (HT – 27 July) – "how Pakistan establishment could afford to embark on suicidal venture that would deepen their economic crisis completely oblivious of popular sentiments. This paradox can only be explained by the fact that it is only a small group of people who virtually own Pakistan". Therefore, a long war threatens to be incredibly costly and could result in painful campaign of attrition. India is unlikely to pursue one so long as it represents the only feasible avenues of pursuing objectives of unlimited aims.

Both India and Pakistan have the military capability to venture out for a limited war. However, fears about the success and effectiveness of such military operations, concern about their escalation and whether India or Pakistan can assure itself that war termination would occur on demand, will deter them to exercise any such option. Further, scope for exercising options for a limited war with restricted aims remained a possibility when nuclear capabilities of both India and Pakistan were ambiguous. However, with the availability of nuclear weapon system with both India and Pakistan, it is appreciated that this super capability will play some role in preventing both the states from directly challenging the each other at a time when neither side is capable of effectively neutralising the opponents deterrence. Infact, availability of this capability should deter both the nations to exercise military options to settle their territorial disputes. Therefore, premeditated conventional wars are unlikely, as the policy relevant for the future is fixed not merely in terms of military capability including nuclear weapons but in the broad and determining terms of political choice. However, being a stronger power, political objectives of India are crucial to determine whether she would like to exercise her aggressive strategic options in comparison to Pakistan? One should not lose sight of a fact that it is disadvantageous for India to fragmentise Pakistan any further, and if ever she attempts to annex any territory through invasion it shall further add to her economic and social problems. Therefore, it will be correct to assume that political imperatives for war at the Indian end are non-existent. In Sultan Shahin's words (HT 27 July 99) Pakistan's dying economy is on artificial respiration being provided by the International Monetary fund (IMF) for the 17th time. Therefore, how a failing state running a 'failed economy' can afford for hugely expensive misadventures. Therefore, lack of political incentives only reinforces the deterrence stability otherwise arising from military incapability on both sides.

As conventional conflicts are judged to be implausible for both political and military reasons, it is assumed that Pakistan has every reason to bleed India through unconventional conflicts in the form of state-supported terrorism and insurgency. Infact, the existence of nuclear capabilities with both the nations has closed other options and clearly enabled Pakistan to support insurgency within India as a means of settling various political differences and wearing India down. Such a strategic move of Pakistan enabled her to exploit India's weakness as a state and operate on the premise that India will not retaliate conventionally for fear of sparking a nuclear holocaust. Such strategies may compel India to play similar game, which will ultimately prove dangerous for the environment of the entire South Asia. India has lost one chance to take the war across the border! It should not be considered her strategic passivity or military weakness, but should be attributed to her decisions taken with much deliberation and partly to her desire to complete the restructuring program without losing sight of ongoing high security competition. Having understood the game plan of Pakistan, probably India has taken a decision not to expand her counter insurgency operations both in Kashmir and her eastern states to include cross border operations of any kind. In fact India has realised that during the last ten years her army has not been able to concentrate on basic conventional military training which is an imperative for any army to remain fit for any eventuality. This aspect remains neglected due to her excessive commitments in fighting insurgency both in J & K and other states. Therefore, it is prudent to restrict the employment of armed forces to reactive operations alone within Indian Territory.

It is vividly clear that India will need to restructure her economic and security environment in the new millennium, if she really wishes to meet the coming challenges in cost effective and pragmatic manner and be as a consequential regional super power. This objective is achievable provided she continues progressing with the growth rate achieved in the recent years. However, the present power status of India presents a curious paradox as the regional predominance has been eroded to some extent by Pakistan's success in bleeding India through success of proxy war launched in J&K. The aspect of regional power being pushed around by an aggressive regional competitor one fifth of her size and potential is, to say the least, a little ludicrous. This state of affair needs to be rectified at the earliest. India should clearly exhibit the 'will to power' if it is to graduate from middle level power to full-fledged world class power. This can be achieved by formulating long term strategies and through pursuing them with relentless determination. Let Pakistan remain seized with her wild fancy desire of recovering Kashmir and continue to neglect services domestic problems that could ultimately threaten her stability from within. It is not a wild dream but in case India, for next ten years continues with her development and restricting programs with least desire for any military adventure, should and could become the third pole along with China and Japan reducing Pakistan competition to a side show.

5

Which way from Kargil ?

S.K Singh

The KARGIL CHAPTER IS OVER. Or perhaps it is not. In India, the coming general elections dominate political thinking and action. In Pakistan, politicians, civil servants, thinkers and writers appear both confused and schizophrenic. They are determined to prove to themselves and to the world that Kargil was a military and diplomatic triumph for them; that the nation must rejoice that its Prime Minister, Mr. Nawaz Sharif, had finally internationalised Kashmir; and that India was now jittery and in a fix!

The Pakistan Foreign Minister, Mr. Sartaj Aziz, asserted that there never was any trust between India and Pakistan, and therefore, there had been no betrayal; that the Lahore process was a "small beginning" which failed to produce tangible results. In Lahore, India had stressed on normalisation first and Kashmir later. Kargil had ensured, according to him, that Kashmir was on the top of the agenda while normalisation would come later. The Shimla accord, Mr. Aziz was clear, must be undone, for in 1972 it was through this accord that India had occupied Pakistani territory on the Line of Control. He alleged again in 1984 and 1988, that India occupied pockets of Pakistani territory. Pakistan must now force India to enter into talks about the entire Kashmir issue. Mr.Sharif had already fulfilled his part of the bargain, reflected in the Clinton – Sharif joint statement. Now the second part, i.e. India's dialogue with Pakistan, had to be fulfilled. To this end, Mr. Aziz insisted that the international community "must force India to the dialogue table."

Not to be outdone, his Foreign Secretary declared from Mecca that the "priorities and conditions" on the Kashmir issue would be set by the world and not by India. All bilateral talks with India in the past had been meaningless and without purpose, for India had always treated such talks as " a tactical ploy." India and Pakistan spoke two different languages. Pakistan spoke the language of peace and India of hegemony and violence. Therefore, the two countries needed the services of an "interpreter".

Can Mirza Aslam Beg called the so-called "sanctity of the LoC" a preposterous theme. India was the "usurper" in Kashmir and could not be permitted to demand that the LoC be made permanent. He asserted that Pakistan had made enormous contributions towards the liberation of Afghanistan from the Russians. "Afghans will now happily repay this debt in Kashmir."

The Americans and Germans felt that Pakistan would be upset with the G-8 statement on Kargil. However, when they were told that the Pakistani Foreign Office had claimed that the "text of the statement suited Pakistan immensely," an American spokesman said, " I cannot understand this. I don't know where the disconnect is." The American added that those who had planned Kargil did not take all the possibilities sufficiently into calculation. Pakistan had planned Kargil in order to underline for India the perils of not solving the overall Kashmir issue. India's response succeeded in underlining the immediate perils Pakistan faced through not solving Kargil on Indian terms. Thus, in this instance, the Kashmir issue refused to get internationlised, even in the face of a major war scare.

Immediately after Mr. Sharif returned from Washington, several Pakistani commentators observed that it might not be easy for any third party to bring enough "persuasive pressure" on a country the size and diplomatic clout of India. Some of them agreed with The New York Times which had commented, that India had shown firmness as well as restraint in its own response to Kargil. India had elected to incur an inordinate number of casualties but refused to act with precipitate desperation or anger.

Lt. Gen. Javed Nasser, Formerly Director-General, Inter-Services Intelligence and Mr. Sharif's Security Adviser in the PMO, a life-long Tablighi, recently wrote something, which should alarm us. Noting that their trusted friend, China, too had asked Pakistan to observe the sanctity of the LoC, he said that gave the LoC the status of a de facto national boundary. He went on to say that Kargil had offered the Pakistan Army the opportunity of a century to redeem its honour and take revenge for Dhaka. This major penetration (in Kargil) by the Pakistan Army would serve as a strong incentive to the Sikhs, giving them the opportunity of the millennium to play havoc with India's lines of communications. These two elements would precipitate the disintegration of India. The Sikh dream of Khalistan, and the Tamil rising in the south, and the Nagas and Mizo tribes in the north-east declaring UDI would lead to India's total desperation when it saw everything being lost. India would then initiate a nuclear war, which might be opposed by some sensible Indian Military commanders. They might even refuse to obey insane orders. He concluded that ultimately the UN Security Council would have to get involved; and sooner or later, India would have to swallow the bitter pill of settling Kashmir on UN terms that were acceptable to Pakistan.

In India, the general elections scheduled for September-October are in; the focus. As has been discussed above, in Pakistan a stranger schizophrenia has overtaken the leadership and the people. There are hints that the top echelons of politicians and military leaders have failed to evolve a consensus; except perhaps on their demand for Kashmir.

The U.S. policy makers are no longer shy of asserting that the era of an even-handed American foreign policy, treating India and Pakistan equally, is over. The time has come for U.S. to pursue separate vectors, trajectories and velocities in its relations with India and Pakistan. They have paid high compliments to the quality and style evolved during the Jaswant Singh – Strobe Talbott series of meetings and discussions by calling these "the most comprehensive and the most extensive exchange of their type" between our countries. In respect of U.S.-India relationship, the assumptions that were firmly held for generations by strategic thinkers stand severely challenged now. India's policy reforms have led to a broad convergence of economic interests between the two countries. The Americans believe that India and Pakistan as nuclear-armed states must not challenge each other militarily and directly; also, they must sort out contentious issues between themselves.

In the face of the current feebleness of the Pakistani economy, its dependence on multilateral aid and its association with all kinds of Islamic militants and doubtful characters like Osama bin Laden, any sort of appreciation or acceptance of Pakistani policies has become difficult to envisage.

One hopes that India's preoccupation with the general elections till September will provide India and Pakistan with time to cool off. If this gives both the countries some breathing time, one could hope for rational discussions and negotiations later on. Also, an opportunity to create the kind and quality of atmosphere in which both sides can make adjustments and concessions and compromises. Otherwise, these two asymmetrical neighbours may be entering a period of mutual benign neglect, even deep indifference. Maintaining this no-war, no-peace situation is bound to create its own problems and tensions. But it appears that Pakistan does not wish to leave us with many options.

But Kashmir isn't the Problem

Pakistan's Kargil operation was directed against India. It was stemmed, though not settled, by an agreement between Pakistan Prime Minister Nawaz Sharif and US President Bill Clinton. India, however, had to drive out the intruders from its territory militarily, achieved though major sacrifices and sustaining major casualties.

Kargil occurred within weeks of Prime Minister AB Vajpayee's bus journey to Lahore. The two Prime Ministers wanted to use the Lahore process for updating and strengthening the 27-year old Simla Agreement, in the context of both countries becoming nuclear weapons pow4ers. Even as some Pakistanis were engaged in drafting and negotiating the Lahore Agreement documents eventually signed in Lahore, much larger numbers of Pakistanis were clandestinely organizing military aggression in Kargil. The aim was to enable Pakistani forces to interdict and block the Srinagar-Leh road, ultimately separate Ladakh from Kashmir, and prevent India from reaching supplies to its forces in Siachen.

In the last two decades, Pakistan has emerged as the principal bully-terrorist nation of South, Southwest and Central Asia. Angrily responding to the Soviet Union's military intervention in Afghanistan in 1979-80, the US made Pakistan the frontline state for organizing Afghan resistance and destroying the Soviet Empire in Central Asia. Finances and armaments worth $ 8 billion flowed in to train and equip Afghan 'freedom fighters' and the Islamic Jehadis.

Pakistan exploited the opportunity to become the main promoter of Islamic fundamentalism and terrorism in the region. Between 1980 and 1988, when Islamabad organised the Afghans to resist and destroy the Soviet Union, Pakistan could do no wrong in the Western eyes. It was, therefore, able to clandestinely acquire considerable nuclear technology, designs and ancillaries. Its premier intelligence Agency, the ISI, which was functioning in Afghanistan and Central Asia, also built intelligence operations of doubtful ethics against India.

The ISI attempted to create a separate Khalistan state. From 1989, Pakistan waged an unrelenting proxy war in J&K. The ISI exfiltrated Kashmiri youth for the training camps in POK, and later infiltrated-trained terrorists back into the state. They were often accompanied by hordes of Afghans, Arabs and Pakistani

Jehadis. The effort was to spread terror even in Indian areas far away from the Pakistan-Indian border.

Pakistan started advertising its nuclear weapons capability sometime in 1986-87. This transformed it into becoming the assertive Big Islamic dada of the region, and unabashedly spread a 'hate-India-destroy – India' message amongst its own people. Their objective was to de-link Kashmir from India, and grab it – and this gradually became their single most persistent political, military and territorial objective.

Over the years the ISI and the Pak Army GHO, rather than the political leadership of Pakistan, acquired the right to manage the nation's policies in respect of both Afghanistan and India. By now the ISI has succeeded in edging out the Pak Foreign Office from these areas of their national policy devising.

Each of Pakistan's conflicts with India (in 1947-48,1965 and 1971) was followed by consultations, leading to their signing a formal document of peace. Until the Kargil contretemps, on all these occasions, India made peace with them, without fuss and rigidity, reflecting a feeling of tolerance and trying to understand the motives of the small neighbour.

India's attitude was that it had more in common with Pakistan than with any other country and, therefore, our policymaker must dare to hope that the two countries will not take up a permanently hostile posture towards each other. The all-important goal was to always impress upon Pakistan that in this complex and not-always-so friendly a world we also share common stakes and interests.

This impelled India to make many unwarranted concessions to Pakistan, hoping for a future of genuine brotherly relations between the two nations. It was in this pursuit that Prime Minister Indira Gandhi decided in 1972 to return 93,000 Pakistani Prisoners of War and approximately 6,000 sq. miles of territory to Pakistan, through the Simla Agreement, without forcing on Bhutto a final and formal settlement of the Kashmir issue, merely on the basis of an oral understanding with him. This understanding Bhutto later ridiculed, publicly asserting that he did not feel committed to anything that he might have signed on a piece of paper in Simla under duress!

As Indian Ambassador in Islamabad during the post-Simla period, I got the first indications from certain Pakistanis in high positions, (one such was Gen Akhtar Abdul Rehman Khan) that they were anxious for revenge against India, for having assisted in what they saw as the secession of Bangladesh from themselves. Pakistan also claimed to have acquired nuclear weapons, as there was a major threat from India to her security!

Against this background, India must henceforth ensure that the ruling establishment in Pakistan does not underestimate India's will and capability to look after its defence. We must never be complacent or unprepared in these matters.

While agreeing to yet another peace arrangement with Pakistan this time, India must consider its timing and terms. Nobody wishes to prescribe any pre-conditions, but we must be clear about the precise meaning of the expression: "Once the sanctity of the line of control has been fully restored" (emphasis added). We are not thinking only of the LoC in Kargil, but of our security across the entire length of the LoC. The full restoration of the sanctity requires us to be assured that all-illegal deliberate violations of the LoC cease; we need to come to an understanding that shelling or shooting across the LoC will end. No further exfiltrations and infiltrations across the LoC shall be permitted. No gun running, and no further narco-terrorism.

We desisted from demanding explicit assurances in our earlier discussions/settlements with Pakistan. In the light of the Kargil experience it would not be wise to remain oblique about our anxieties. The two countries need to assume reciprocal responsibilities and obligations in these matters. We have to maintain peace, and ensure stability of borders. We must test Pakistan's sincerity in structuring cooperation with us. Today's technology and the multinational involvement in terrorism practiced in Afghanistan has made terrorism big business, backed-up by big money, huge arms and equipment supplies, with the backing of private, quasi religious groups.

After our general elections, we will need consultations; perhaps negotiations to devise stable India-Pakistan bilateral relations, with a clear understanding of border management. Devising peaceful bilateral relationship must be made mutually beneficial. The Nawaz Sharif – Clinton joint statement could be a first step towards the return of peace and quiet in Kargil and the entire LoC. We need to check out the precise perceptions of the USA about this. India must make any further promotion of cross-border terrorism expensive and unattractive. We have been providing Pakistan evidence about its involvement in promoting terrorism in India. Henceforth, we will have to be even more candid and blunt.

We recognise that Pakistan has used the Kargil incident to re-agitate the so-called "core" issue of

Kashmir. The apprehension in Indian mind, and the hope in many Pakistani hearts, is that the Americans will back their effort to impose a settlement of the Kashmir issue. Few in India believe that the Kashmir issue is the real problem. Today, the real issue is Pakistan's desire to persist with its prejudices and complexes, born of an amalgam of envy and contempt and a yearning for revenge.

The problems of Kashmir ultimately need to be settled by the people of India, not by Pakistan or other outsiders.

Talks with Islamabad Till After the Elections.

Guns are no longer booming in the Kargil-Drass-Batalik sectors of north Kashmir. India and the world watched Pakistani troops as they vacated Indian Territory. International pressures, Pakistan's apprehension of losing multilateral economic assistance and the persistent valor of the Indian Army combined to achieve this. Pakistan's promise of vacating this region has been fulfilled.

Negotiations usually start once the fighting dies down. The joint statement signed by United States President Bill Clinton and Pakistan Prime Minister Nawaz Sharif after their July 4 meeting has suggested that the process of bilateral dialogue envisaged in Lahore in February this year is resumed.

The prospect for this may not be bright immediately. Pakistan keeps on insistent that Kashmiri Mujahideen (freedom Fighters), and not Pakistani troops, had crossed the Line of Control. They would like the world, and India, to believe that their army personnel were not involved and that, the Pakistan government had little control over the fighters in Kargil. Also that these Kashmiri Mujahids are not amenable to Pakistani discipline. The Pakistan government, through all these false assertions, wishes to imply also that its army has not tasted defeat in Kargil.

Some of the Islamic fundamentalist Mujahids assert that they will not go from Kashmir, as Kashmiris cannot be asked to leave their own country. India certainly has never accepted this specious line of argument. Neither do a number of other countries. India has collected considerable evidence to show that 80 to 90 percent of those who had crossed the LOC from Pakistan-occupied Kashmir(POK) were regular Pakistan Army soldiers belonging to the Northern Light Infantry of the Pakistani 10 Corps.

When an entire society is exposed repeatedly to an oft-repeated falsehood, and this keeps being parroted over decades, they ultimately come to believe that their falsehood must indeed be the truth. And, if there is nobody to contradict this from within the society, then it becomes a truth that people do not dare to question or doubt.

That Kashmir must belong to Pakistan; that India was committed to a plebiscite in Kashmir, that India has kept the Muslims of Kashmir under its brutal military heel through the power of its guns; that this has involved Pakistan; Self –evident, uncontested, unquestionably true facts, believed universally in that country.

We know, and the world knows, that the training, arming, financing and equipping of all varieties of Arabs, Afghan – Talibans, Pakistani Pushtoons and others have been undertaken by the Inter-Services Intelligence (ISI) for decades. Large numbers of serving and retired colonels and generals – such as Gen. Hamid Gul, the former ISI Chief - believe that Pakistan is fully justified in arming, training and infiltrating these guerrillas into India.

Also, at the same time, they wish us to believe that Pakistan's assistance to them has merely been diplomatic, political and ideological. Nothing more material or concrete. Their logic goes thus: Pakistan is Muslim, so are Kashmiris; and, therefore, India, as a non-Muslim entity, must and shall quit Kashmir. All that Islamabad needs to do in this context is to sustain the Kashmir issue until the inevitable happens, i.e. Kashmir falling into Pakistan's lap.

Since the fighting commenced in Kargil, Pakistan has made every effort to start a substantive discussion with India on the eventual settlement of the Kashmir issue. It wishes to evade a discussion on Kargil and insists on discussing the larger Kashmir dispute. India, on the other hand, wishes to discuss only the departure of Pakistani soldiers and other miscreants from Kargil, and not the Kashmir issue.

There have been some back channel contacts between India and Pakistan, and these have muddied the waters somewhat. Early in this tragic business, Pakistan provided former ambassador to India, Niaz Naik, a special aircraft to fly to New Delhi for a day. He stated on the BBC that he had met with Prime Minister Atal Behari Vajpayee and that he proposed a discussion between the Pakistani and Indian directors general of military operations (DGMOs) to work out the modalities of winding down the fighting. He also claimed to have discussed the idea of a safe corridor for the withdrawal of Pakistanis from Kargil.

This indicated to the world that Pakistan was ready to withdraw its forces from the LOC. For this, they sought a cease-fire, which was not agreed to. At this stage, Pakistan also made public the fact that senior Indian journalist R.K. Mishra had earlier visited Lahore for a discussion with Sharif.

As regards the resumption of bilateral dialogue under the Lahore process, Brajesh Mishra, the principal Secretary to the Prime Minister, has stated that this can happen only after a total withdrawal of Pakistan forces. Foreign Minister Jaswant Singh has separately laid down clear conditionalities. One, Pakistan must abide by its commitment to withdraw its troops completely by a given date. Two, it must undertake to stop sponsoring cross-border terrorism and demonstrate that it committed to maintaining the sanctity of the LOC. If the sanctity of the LOC has to be maintained, there should be no violations through the smuggling in, or out, of groups of persons, or arms, or any other unlawful movement.

Indeed, common sense suggests that between now and September only the contacts considered unavoidable between the two countries shall take place; and that, too, on non-fundamental issues. Talks on fundamental or really weighty matters must follow later, after the Indian general election, which will end in early October.

Vajpayee's historic bus to Lahore in February 1999 was hijacked – and diverted to Kargil. Clearly, even as Vajpayee was visiting Lahore, Pakistan was making preparations clandestinely to give India a black eye in Kargil.

The people of India are convinced that all this was part of a deliberate charade and deception. India while demonstrating its goodwill and friendliness received a kick in the teeth. Pakistan has acted in secrecy and with malice. India has serious doubts about Pakistan's intentions. And it is unable to demonstrate its usual soft visage of tolerance and mutual trust.

Focus on Kashmir – Pakistan's Foreign Policy

Since Independence and partition, Pakistan has been a difficult neighbour with whom our links have been many and close. China after 1962 saw Pakistan as a close friend, who deserved help. During the cold war period, the West was glad to have it as a protégé, able and willing to render services.

Pakistan has tried to grab Kashmir ever since the partition, believing that as a predominantly Muslim state, it must wish to join them. Its efforts to annex Kashmir have followed the same unvarying route, tricks and technique: What they first tried in October 1947, was repeated on each subsequent occasion – May 1948, July-September 1965, and autumn 1998 onwards in Kargil. Each time, they began by sending their army personnel in mufti, claiming that these were either tribals, or true- believing Islamists, or fervent, Mujahideen- Jehadis, or members of Kashmir liberation movement; or Taliban from neighbouring Afghanistan; indeed anything but what they are. Each time they have denied connections with the Pakistan army and each time these claims have proved false.

Sir Mohammed Zafarullah Khan, their very first Foreign Minister, had to confess in the Security Council that regular Pakistan army elements were indeed involved; and this has been repeated in 1965 and 1971. In his recent interaction with Nawaz Sharif, President Clinton indicated that he believed that Pak regulars were involved in the Kargil problem. The world is refusing to believe that unknown to the ISI and Pakistani army, it was the Lashkar-e-Tayyaba and Harkat –ul-Ansar and other Islamist – Jehadis from inside and outside Pakistan who fought in the Kargil – Drass-Batalik areas. When asked how these Kashmiri youth have received access to snow mobiles, heavy artillery etc at these Himalayan heights of 14 to 18 thousand feet, Pakistan shrugs and has no reply to give.

Bhutto once said that the Pakistan army was the country's protective "wolf hound, always on duty, powerful enough to keep the enemy at bay, or to destroy its 'Master', if the latter forget the proper password or the hound's feeding hour". Nothing, not even Simla could discourage Bhutto. He asserted after 1972 that "India.......thrust upon us violence, tyranny and oppression....... denied to the Pakistanis the plebiscite that had been pledged". And he commented later that Simla was "to his mind, irrelevant as far as Kashmir is concerned"....... No matter what was written on a piece of paper he may have signed; "he had not accepted Indian position, Indira Gandhi's position". In recent years several Pakistani politicians, commentators, army and diplomats have declared unilaterally that Simla does not and cannot bind or commit Pakistan.

In another manner, too, the pattern each time has been repetitive. After each time's fighting, Pakistan tends to lose its principal dramatis personae. In the midst of the 1947-49 fighting, they faced the demise of a frustrated Jinnah through anxiety and ill health. In another few years, Liaquat Ali Khan was assassinated.

After 1965-66 the country saw the sacrifice of Field Marshal Ayub Khan who had to quit ignominiously, after his peers told him to quit the Presidency. The wider war of 1971 resulted not only in the separation of Bangladesh, but also Bhutto's execution soon thereafter.

Pakistanis blamed him for his political failure, and lack of understanding of the psychology of his own armed forces and his political peers who were from other parties. Bhutto paid with his life for having made himself the nation's buffer between the society at large and the army. Once the army under Zia had taken over governance, and claimed that it alone represented the entire society, the buffer had to be destroyed, as an awkward piece of evidence of the schizophrenia that is Pakistan.

In the last ten years the Pakistan army and politicians have underlined the importance of Kashmir and raised its international profile. Along side, Pakistani Islam has been evolving. The present generation of Pakistani leaders in politics, military, business and industry have used Islam as their faith, and as their society's principal motivation for using both Islamic urges and frustrations, as also the Islamic fervour, not only nationally but also in the entire region i.e. in Afghanistan, Iran and Central Asia. They exploited this for promoting, their own Kashmir – related agenda. They made a conscious effort to identify the entire region's Islam with militancy in Kashmir, and thereafter claim that the army and the Jamaati-Jehadi groups are spearheading the Islamic urges for Pakistan's future.

Mixing Islam with liberation in Afghanistan, Pakistan was able to strengthen and enrich its own army and ISI at the expense of those who wanted merely to damage the Soviets. The stocks of arms they gained in

Afghanistan have been exploited ever since for their so-called Jehad in Kashmir. The army and the ISI, therefore, claim that they, and not the Pakistani foreign office, should handle decision-making in respect of the country's Kashmir and Afghanistan policies. Also that policies in the nuclear and missile contexts should remain their exclusive preserve.

The tripod of decision-makers that ran Pakistan after Zia's death consisted of the President, Prime Minister and the Chief of Army Staff. The tripod ruled supreme, until Nawaz Sharif with his two third majority in the National Assembly was able to knock out, first the President and later the Chief Justice followed by General Jehangir Karamat. This sent a firm message down to the military, and to the country that henceforth this PM intended to exercise state authority by himself, in a style that should be called monolithic. It is probable that the Kargil incident has been used by the army for reinventing itself, due to its greed for power. Its involvement, through the ISI with narcotics big money, small arms and terrorism all over the region, gave it a de facto leadership amongst all the drug-money-small arms mafias in the region.

In recent months, the US, Saudi Arabia, Pakistan and the Afghan Taliban have had their different anxieties about Osama bin Laden and his select band of crackpot terrorists. This must have been a factor in sensitising the US to the dangers inherent in their trusting the Pak army. The US oil companies too have been getting worried about the capacity of the Taliban with Pakistani help, to bottle up and keep unutilised the hydrocarbon resources of Central Asian Countries. The US has thus acquired a new insight into the affairs of the Taliban in Afghanistan. Saudis and Iranians too have seen through

Pakistan's negative role vis-à-vis their own efforts through the OIC to seek greater Shia-Sunni coordination. These factors have opened the eyes of many around the world about the depth of irrationality in Pakistani policies, beliefs and ideas.

The Islamic factor in Sinkiang too is now beginning to bubble over. Brooding over all these elements and factors is the nuclear and missile capability of Pakistan that is irresponsible as also difficult. Can Nawaz Sharif face up to the complexities of real life in this extremely complex geopolitical and geoeconomic environment? Are relations between Pakistan, its army, and their old and tried allies, China and the US, likely to remain simple and unwavering or are we seeing the contours of a volatile and dangerous new set of perceptions?

Too few in Delhi and Islamabad remember today that JFK had sent Ambassador Chester Bowles for the second time to Delhi in succession to Ambassador Galbraith for just one purpose, that of getting India replace Pakistan as the US' predominant partner in South Asia. The cold war, however, was still raging and the State Department and the Pentagon were above to get the President to review his earlier determination, and not abandon Pakistan. Again, in 1966, at the Tashkent summit when Lal Bahadur Shastri and Ayub Khan met for the first time, by themselves, but with Prime Minister Kosygin present; Shastri told Ayub in his typically unvarnished and plain style: "You may not like to hear this, Mr. President. But you should not expect me to give you Kashmir as a gift". This has not changed.

6

The Kargil Misadventure

Arun Bhagat

The events of May to July 1999 will be remembered for a long time to come. The repercussions will last even longer. A coalition government concerned and preoccupied with the forthcoming elections is informed in bits and pieces, that Indian Territory has been occupied. The enemy is in possession of vital peaks and is well entrenched. They are in our own bunkers and are well armed and equipped. They are at higher altitudes and have a natural advantage. Heavy casualties should be expected and if they defend well, removing them physically will be time-consuming process. They have crept in silently, surreptitiously. Not a single bullet has been fired and not a single sentinel has been injured. It is weeks before citizens of the country learn about the full dimensions of the intrusions.

This was not the time for recriminations. Nor was it the time to find fault or apportion blame. There would be time enough for that. The Motherland must be cleared of the enemy first. Whatever the cost! The directions are clear and are fully understood. The drills, the sweat and tears of training, the pride, devotion, love of country, determination and courage

once again come to the aid of the Nation. The enemy is slowly but surely rolled back. The sacrifices are heavy. The young warriors have yet again kept their pledge to the Mother. They die to live up to the oath they took reverentially, clasping the National flag in their hands.
Lt. General Akhtar Hussain Malik, GOC 12 Division of Pakistan, in the year 1965, conceived operation Gibraltar. General Ayub Khan had by then reorganized the Army, purchased new armaments, conducted exercises to test the newly introduced command and control systems. Intrusion into Kutch had succeeded. He was confident and gave the green signal to the operation. Under it 6000 to 8000 infiltrators were sent into Kashmir. The people of Jammu and Kashmir were supposed to rise up in revolt. As in 1947, it was not to be. The invaders were all killed. Every single one of them. The misadventure led to the September, 1965 war.

The Kargil intrusion is a repeat performance. Attributed to General Azizzuddin it was formulated in 1994 to cut off the supply lines to the Siachin glacier. The Lahore declaration had not been well received in Pakistan. Every motive was being attributed to Nawaz Sharif. The state of the economy was dismal and unlike India the suspension of aid and loans had hit Pakistan hard and stifled the economy. The national debt had risen to Rs.2880 billion against a GNP of Rs.2,760 billion. Of this the foreign debt component was US $ 28.6 billion. The exchange rate of a dollar had risen to 52 Pak rupees. The index of the Karachi Stock Market was at its lowest. No new listing had taken place for 6 months. There had been a shortfall in wheat production and over U.S $ 1 billion was required for wheat imports alone. Foreign exchange reserves were down to the same amount. Debt servicing had become a recurring problem. Sectarian strife was increasing by the day. The Ahle Sunnat projected by the Barreilivies and the Ahle Hadis representing the Deobandis were at each other's throats. Islamabad had brought Sind under direct central rule without any improvement. Terrorist groups like Harkut ul ansar, Sipah Salar, Lashkar- e – Toiba, which had been given virtual recognition by the State and worked closely with the Army and its intelligence wing, were getting out of control. They had built up linkages with powerful Generals. The Army was unhappy. They had not approved of the Lahore declaration, which did not even mention Kashmir or UN resolutions. Amidst this gloom emerged this audacious prospect of occupying vital peaks across the LOC. Nature appeared to favor the adventure. The snows had been mild. The patrolling patterns had been closely watched. There were no patrols worth the name. The Indians would not come near till the end of April or May. By the time the Indian defences could be strengthened and they would be given a complete tactical surprise. The Tanzeems would get busy along with the Army. The opposition would be silenced and the people would be jubilant. A liberated zone could be declared. With Pakistan a nuclear power, the western world and China would step in. Material support would pour in from Islamic countries. Early detection could always lead to withdrawal. The same ruse of shrugging off all responsibility would be used. If they did not succeed the Government stand was clear. After all it had been effectively adopted innumerable times before. If the Mujahidin succeeded and a liberated zone was formed even for a short period, everyone would know who was behind the victory. Either way this diversion would relieve pressures on the Pakistani Government. World pressure, the possibility of a larger nuclear conflagration, would leave the caretaker coalition Government in India with limited options. An all win situation was perceived.

However, this was not to be! The Indian response was swift and unexpected. The use of fighter aircrafts added a new dimension. The determination with which men and supplies were rushed gave a clear message of intentions and capabilities. The sheer fury of the assaults on well held defensive positions, unmindful of the casualties and despite the loss of three aircrafts within the first two days, upset all these presumptions. The Indian Army caught unawares had a point to prove. They had to redeem themselves. A rapid reappraisal, forceful tactics, innumerable acts of individual and group valor, the interdiction caused by aircraft and artillery was too much to withstand. The tide turned rapidly.

There is disquiet and consternation as to how and why this could happen. How could such large numbers cross well guarded borders over a period of months with arms, ammunition, food, building materials and settle down undetected. The inroads were up to 12 kilometers in many places. This in an area which has been a hot bed for the past 5\7 years with regular exchanges of artillery and mortar fire. Kargil town and the National highway had been targeted from across the border. Strategic intelligence is important in both war and peace. In Jammu and Kashmir we have a unique situation. We have war in peace. Intelligence is received in bits and pieces. Rarely is it the whole apple. Analysts put these pieces together. They rely on tactical intelligence as well. Some slivers were forthcoming as early as May \ June 1998. In the latter part of the same year reports were received and disseminated. It appears that the Northern Command took over 10 days to fully fathom and understand the gravity of the situation. Army Headquarters would naturally rely on their assessments. Not often those tasked with analysis interact closely with officers in the field. This interaction has its uses but also has its pitfalls. The terrorist outfits involved have claimed that they had moved across the LOC last year itself. All the indications are that the Pakistani movement took place early this year. The snows had been mild. The original plan could have been modified to expand the area, increase the strengths and take over more peaks because it proved to be easy. The Indians failed to detect the Pakistanis. They could well have originally envisaged it as a swift operation of interdiction causing heavy damage, disrupting the vital supply route. The hospitable conditions would have added to their confidence. A senior Army officer serving in the area in an interview has attributed the happenings to intelligence failure. The Press has reported Army officers having admitted that they received stray reports about plans of infiltration into Kashmir using the Kargil route. No reference was however made to occupation, it is reported. It cannot be the contention that a different type of vigil was required. The forces deployed have their tasks clearly defined. Their deployment is to interdict all movement across the border. As many as 16 Pakistani Tanzeems apart from the Pakistan Army had taken part in the Kargil misadventure. Preparations had been afoot for some time. Extra snow clothing and specialized equipment was purchased in Europe. Such indicators are sought by intelligence agencies. It is clear that these indicators were missed or if available were not pieced together. Lack of strategic intelligence could have been made up by the observations on the ground through scouts and patrols. The Brigade Commander had sought satellite and air reconnaissance in 1998. Let us not forget that two shepherds observed the Pakistanis first and reported their presence to the forces. They had one pair of binoculars between them. Purposeful and planned patrolling would certainly have revealed the presence of 1500\2000 troops spread over an area of about 1400 square kilometers even if their ingress was not contemporaneously detected much earlier.

The version put out by Pakistan was not found acceptable by anyone. It was clear from the beginning that it was beyond the capability of terrorist groups to undertake such a massive operation at heights of 15000 feet and above. Proof of the direct involvement of Pakistani troops was soon available in ample measure. World reaction was as categorical and emphatic, as the position taken by India .The U.S.A, the G-8, the European Union all told Pakistan to withdraw it troops and to restore the sanctity of the LOC. Ruffled at the unanimous and severe adverse reaction of the world leaders and the rumblings within the country Nawaz Sharif rushed to China almost in the same manner that Yahya Khan had sent Air Marshal Asgar Khan in 1971. The reception was cool. The Pak PM was told to settle the matter bilaterally. His request to stop over in New Delhi was firmly turned down. New Delhi had already afforded an escape route to Nawaz. The Indian perception made public was that the Pakistan Prime Minister had not been privy to the Kargil incursions. New Delhi did not find any justification to lend a further helping hand. Pakistani requests for a visit to New Delhi of their Foreign Minister were also met coolly. The brief visit when it materialized was expectedly infructuous. The Blair House declaration of the 4th of July 1999 is one of its kind. .Unlike Camp David only one party was a signatory along with the guarantor. India was not present but was consulted and her point of view accepted. The determination on the battlefield, adroit diplomacy, the decision not to cross the LOC, preparations for a longer and larger conflict had proved effective. The world and Pakistani understood the message clearly. Pakistan started withdrawing its forces and the so-called Mujahiddin.

Nawaz Sharif now faces unprecedented hostility at home. The Kargil misadventure has been dubbed variously as a fiasco, a debacle, defeat, and humiliation. The country is now engaged in grave introspection. Pakistan's press is recalling the complete litany of blunders starting with the dispatch of thousands of ill trained, ill-equipped tribesmen with Pakistani troops into Kashmir in October, 1947. This had left the Maharaja with no alternative but to sign the treaty of accession with India with the support of the dominant political parties. The incursion into Kutch, the dispatch of raiders into Kashmir again in August 1965,the follies of 1971 and the abject surrender of 100,000 Pakistani troops are all being recalled. Air Marshal Asgar Khan says the past wars with India had been fought for no purpose and Pakistan had suffered humiliation in each one of them. The failures are attributed to incompetent leadership, weak and infirm institutions. Some Pakistani articles have candidly praised the manner in which the Indian caretaker Government handled the situation and the institutional strengths of the country. The misadventure has cost Pakistan dearly. One can only hope some lessons will be learnt and some change in the Pakistani mindset takes place.

Yet, Kargil, has been just one more episode in Pakistani policy towards India that has had a fixed focus irrespective of the party or the military dictator in power. "Moral and diplomatic", support to the Mujahadin is an integral part of this policy. The world has come to realize that these are euphemisms for planning, coordinating, supporting terrorist activities in India. The activities have not been restricted to Jammu and Kashmir terrorist groups. They have been guiding, assisting, supplying arms, ammunition, explosives, and funds to fundamentalists and rabid elements all over India. They have demonstrated special affinity for criminals & the drug Mafia. The intimate relationship of the ISI with drug cartels within and outside Pakistan has proved to be useful. The hand of Pakistani agencies in the Bombay bomb blasts, Sardar Beant Singh's assassination, the attempt on the life of General Krishna Rao, the Governor of Jammu and Kashmir, to cite a few examples, have been fully established. There are scores of other instances in which from the stage of conception, training, funds and the preparation of devices in laboratory conditions, Pakistani agencies have been involved. Punjab suffered for long years from Pakistani organized terrorism. The many bilateral exchanges at different levels in the past, the joint statements issued from time to time, did not in any way alter the Pakistani objective to spread terrorism using fundamentalists, criminals and any and all other means. Kashmir is merely a convenient cover. The real Pakistani agenda is widely different and more pernicious. Opposition to India has become a creed. India is blamed for the dismemberment of Pakistan. It is also blamed for the efforts of the Muslim migrants (Mohajirs) to Pakistan, for attempting to get space and recognition. Whether it is the lesser or the greater politician, the Mullah of the mofussil mosque or one of the many Amirs or the Press the refrain is the same. Strangely, the root cause of India's involvement in the Bangladesh freedom movement in 1971 is forgotten. Their own leaders responsible for the 1971 debacle and those of Bangladesh, who organised the freedom struggle against Pakistan, have been forgiven. The Lahore declaration could not and did not change the position. And the Kargil misadventure was very much in conformity with the avowed Pakistani policy towards India.

7

Kargil- The Pakistan Gamble

Major General Afsir Karim (Retd.)

The roots of the Kargil episode can be traced back to Pakistan's frustration in failing to engineer a people's revolt in Kashmir. The people of Kashmir, despite coercion by terrorists, opted for an elected government in 1996. Tired of the continued violence instigated by Pakistan sponsored terrorist groups, people opted for peace. Pakistan, in desperation, opted for military action and dangerous brinkmanship in Ladakh. Pakistan violated the well-established LOC in Kargil sector against the terms of the Simla (now Shimla) agreement signed between India and Pakistan after the 1971 war (see Annexure1.1.)

In accordance with the Simla Agreement, the sanctity of the Line of Control was to be maintained by both sides. The relevant extract (para 4[ii]) of the agreement reads:

Neither side shall seek to alter it [the LOC] unilaterally, irrespective of mutual differences and legal interpretations. Both sides further undertake to refrain from threat or use of force in violation of this Line.

After the Simla agreement, designated military commanders of India and Pakistan delineated the Line of Control, indicating the position of the two armies on the day of cease-fire. The delineation of the LOC was finalised after detailed surveys, several discussions and identification on the ground. Maps showing the LOC were signed by the military commanders of both countries to endorse the agreement on the LOC (see Annexure 1.2). Both the Indian and Pakistani governments accorded approval to the joint recommendations submitted by their respective military commanders. Consequently, on 20 December 1972, a joint statement by India and Pakistan paved the way for withdrawal of troops to their sides of the international border and the Line of Control in Kashmir.

The position now taken by Pakistan in regard to the LOC is not tenable. It goes to show that Pakistan no longer wants to adhere to the Simla Agreement. The violation of the LOC by large bodies of troops amount to an act of belligerence and annulment of the Shimla Agreement. Pakistan has once again embarked on an armed invasion in Kashmir in preference to negotiations. The armed intrusions across the LOC have brought about a qualitative change in the situation in Kashmir, which is bound to have far-reaching effects on the future of Indo-Pak relations. Unprovoked-armed action in Ladakh by Pakistan has opened the gates of confrontation and conflict.

In the past, disagreements over the alignment of the LOC between local military commanders were settled after a few 'flag meetings', even after clashes or exchange of fire between troops. This may no longer be possible because of the hardened attitudes and bitterness created by the unprovoked mini war at Kargil.

Operations in Kargil

The aggression across the LOC in Kargil clearly indicated a well-planned military operation with a view to capture territory across the LOC, which would provide a springboard for further offensive operations inside Indian Kashmir.

An operation of this magnitude could only be planned at the highest level in Pakistan with complete approval of the government. Regular troops were grouped with Afghan war veterans and specially trained Islamist groups for this operation. A reconstruction of the events and pattern of deployment of Pak troops shows that three brigade groups were ordered to launch operations from Dras to Turtuk. Each brigade launched three special groups, as follows.

* 62 [Pak] Brigade located at Skardu provided one group for crossing the LOC at Batalik.

* 82 [Pak] Brigade located at Minimarg was to provide a group for Kargil-Dras sectors.

* 232 [Pak] Brigade located at Dansam was to launch operations across the LOC in Turtuk, south of Siachen glacier.

Each group was provided artillery, engineering and logistic support by the respective brigades.

All the groups were supported by elements of Pakistan's Special Service Group (SSG) comprising highly specialised commando troops of the Pakistan Army.

The main phases and objectives of the offensive appeared to be as follows:

PHASE I

* Designated groups wee to occupy unheld areas or those vacated by the Indian Army during winter by stealth in Chorbat La, Batalik, Kaksar, Dras and Mushkoh valley.

* Interdiction of the Srinagar-Leh road (The national highway, NH 1A) between Dras and Kargil by artillery fire and physical occupation wherever possible.

* Attack on Turtuk to facilitate operations in the Shyok Valley against logistic bases supplying Siachen.

PHASE II

* Highly trained mercenaries supported by SSG elements were to enter Kashmir Valley across the great Himalayan Range to create disturbances and subvert the administration.

* Prepare the ground for the occupation of the Pahalgam – Anantnag belt in the Valley.

PHASE III

* 'Liberation' of Sonamarg, Pahalgam and Anantnag districts by irregular forces led by Afghan war veterans and Pakistan Army troops posing as mujahideen.

PHASE IV

* 'liberation' of the Doda-Kishtwar belt by armed mercenaries.

* Cutting of logistic support routes to Siachen.

It was expected that operations in the Valley and Doda would catch the Indian Army on the wrong foot, as most Army formations would now be engaged in Kargil sector. It was hoped that UN intervention at this stage would become inevitable. In this situation, Pakistan would bargain from a position of strength and largely achieve its political objectives in Kashmir.

This operational plan was obviously over ambitious and unrealistic as Pakistan was in no position to dislodge the Kargil brigade or stop reinforcements from reaching this area. No major operations can be sustained beyond Kargil, much less across the Great Himalayan Range without the capture of Kargil. Mercenaries and terrorists could, however, be infiltrated in greater number into the Kashmir Valley and Doda-Kistwar area. The determination of the Indian Army and its capacity to reorganize rapidly after being surprised at Kargil was obviously underestimated by the Pakistani Higher Command.

In Kargil sector, fierce battles raged, and the Pakistani forces were slowly but surely pushed out of Indian Kashmir. The Pakistani troops operating across the LOC were identified to be from the 2nd, 3rd, 4th, 5th and 6th Battalions of the Northern Light Infantry. These battalions were augmented by Afghan war veterans and Islamic militants trained by the Lashkar-e-taiba and Harkat-ul-Mujahideen, etc. Twenty artillery batteries provided supporting fire for the offensive. The strength and the location of the Pak forces were estimated to be as follows.

* A composite group of 250 at Batalik.
* A composite group of 100 at Kaksar.
* A composite group of 250 at Dras.
* A composite group of 300 in Muskho valley.

A reserve of at least two regular army battalions and a large number of mercenaries were kept ready at various launching areas on the Pakistani side of the LOC. Approximately 2,000 terrorists and well-armed insurgents were to be infiltrated into Kashmir from various points of the LOC into the Kashmir Valley.

It is quite evident that Pakistan's intrusion across the LOC and its expression of doubt about the alignment of the LOC on the ground were part of a predetermined plan. The so-called mujahideen, who were only a part of this plan, were not Kashmiris, but outsiders.

The fallout of the Kargil Imbroglio

Pakistan's violation of the LOC was blatant and without any provocation from India. India and its army had, on the other hand, been lulled into a false sense of security after the Lahore Agreement. Pakistan's naked aggression and violation of the LOC was a result of long and meticulous planning. Pakistan, however, tried to confuse the issue by declaring that it had no involvement in the armed intrusions in Kargil. Pakistan wanted the world to believe that Kashmiri freedom fighters were waging a war against India in which Pakistan had no role. Pakistan's artillery support to the intruders was explained as a normal response to Indian artillery fire across the LOC.

The involvement of the armed forces, the strength of the forces, the sophisticated equipment and the organisation of logistic support, soon made every country of the world realise that in this case Pakistan could not offer any plausible denial, and its involvement was too obvious to be ignored. The USA was the first country to ask Pakistan to withdraw its forces from

Indian Kashmir. Later, the G8 countries, Russia, Japan and even China demanded withdrawal of Pakistani forces to their own side of the LOC. Pakistan's contention that the LOC had never been clearly defined on the ground, and that the Pakistani Army was operating on its own side of the LOC, did not wash. Not many countries accepted this position, and most persisted in their demand for withdrawal of Pakistani forces and cease-fire. To Pakistan's consternation, the UN did not intervene, nor did any country show an inclination to intervene or mediate.

Pakistan, however, continued to trot out the usual excuse that it had no control over the mujahideen operating across the LOC. Pakistan stood isolated and faced the prospects of denial of the IMF loan, which was due to come to it. Pakistan ultimately had to yield ground because of strong international reactions and accept a plan for withdrawal.

Pakistan has somehow always denied its involvement in Kashmir. In 1947-48, it was said that the 'tribal' invasion of Kashmir was a spontaneous reaction of Pathans to save their Muslim brethren from marauding Dogra troops. The memoirs of several generals published later, however, gave details of the objectives and plans made by Maj. Gen. Akbar Khan of the Pakistan Army who conducted the operation called Op Gulmarg under the assumed name 'Gen. Tariq", a legendary figure of Islamic history. In 1965, when large columns of the Pakistani Army infiltrated into the Kashmir Valley, Pakistan feigned innocence and declared that local Kashmiris had revolted against the Indian government, and that Pakistan was in no way involved. But the cover was blown when a full-scale war broke out between India and Pakistan. The operational orders issued to the Pakistan Army for infiltration in various parts of Kashmir, code-named Op Gibraltar, were captured by the Indian Army, and presented later at the UN by the Indian representative to prove the Pakistan Army's involvement.

Pakistan continues to deny any involvement in the proxy war it has been waging in Kashmir since 1989, although the role of the ISI (Inter-Services Intelligence) in training and launching of terrorist-insurgent groups has been quite obvious and evident to most countries. The Kargil episode has blown apart all Pakistani pretensions of non-involvement in the proxy war of Kashmir.

The reasons behind the denial of its role from 1947 onwards are the same. Pakistan cannot possible justify its armed invasion or intrusion in Kashmir. It is obviously not sure of the justness of such a course. Many nations have encouraged and supported Pakistan to create trouble in Indian Kashmir and have readily accepted the Pakistani version because of their own geostrategic interests in Pakistan and Kashmir.

This posture, which is a legacy of the Cold War period, can no longer be justified. Today, it is not Pakistan vs. India, it is a confrontation between secular forces and moderate Muslims of South and Central Asia and Islamic fundamentalists armed and trained in Afghanistan and Pakistan.

India's stand and reactions

After the initial shock and disbelief, India acted swiftly and purposefully. The army was ordered to evict the Pakistan forces without crossing the LOC. Pakistan was told firmly, "withdraw first, talks later". It was also made clear that India would not accept outside intervention or mediation. India's policy to confine the confrontation to its own side of the LOC in Kargil was widely acclaimed by the international community. India's resolve to evict the intruders was considered just, and the restraint shown by the Indians was appreciated.

India's decision to limit the scope of operations in Kargil by not crossing the LOC despite suffering greater losses in the process was calculated not to enlarge the conflict or provide an excuse to Pakistan to seek UN intervention. The Indian Army proved that it was a highly disciplined and professional force as it took this restriction in its stride and forged ahead.

However, Pakistan's unprovoked aggression and efforts to hoodwink the world have caused great anger in India. For the first time in the last 50 years, the Indian masses want their government to crush Pakistan. This resentment is widespread and likely to grow with time unless Pakistan stops meddling in Kashmir. Being a democracy, no government can ignore these sentiments and upsurge against Pakistan, and this may cost Pakistan dear in the long run. Pakistan has refused the hand of friendship offered by India in Lahore and deceived India and the world regarding its real intentions, while promising peace in Lahore, it was simultaneously planning the Kargil operations in great secrecy.

The root cause of the conflict is no longer Kashmir, but the sway of fundamentalists in Pakistan. The question arises whether the US and other secular countries are capable of curbing Islamic terrorism in this region. India can hardly be expected to watch helplessly while Islamic fundamentalists wage overt and covert wars in Kashmir. Taliabanisation and chaotic conditions with Pakistan can make the danger of a nuclear war quite real in South Asia.

The prospects of peace between India and Pakistan are presently bleak. Efforts for peace are not likely to succeed because Islamic militants and fanatics of the Taliban variety who consider themselves soldiers of Allah, are not rational beings and cannot be trusted to maintain peace. Terrorists, insurgents and mercenaries will thrive under their dispensation and democratic processes may not be allowed to continue in Pakistan. Monolithic domination by fanatics of any variety in the strategically sensitive areas of Afghanistan – Pakistan, Central Asia and Kashmir conjures up a frightening scenario.

Peace Initiatives

On 4 July, a Sunday, President Clinton met Mr. Nawaz Sharif in Washington and succeeded in 'convincing' him that it was vital for peace in South Asia that the Line of Control in Kashmir be respected. Mr. Nawaz Sharif agreed that concrete steps would be taken for the restoration of the LOC in accordance with the Simla Agreement.

During the Clinton-Sharif meeting, an inference could be drawn that Nawaz Sharif had agreed to withdraw his forces from Indian-controlled Kashmir and restore status quo ante: the position as it existed before Pakistan's aggression in Kargil sector across the LOC.

The US president and the Prime Minister of Pakistan agreed that the bilateral dialogue begun in Lahore in February 1999 provided the best forum for resolving all issues dividing India and Pakistan, including Kashmir. President Clinton also stated that he would take personal interest in encouraging an expeditious resumption and intensification of those bilateral efforts once the sanctity of the Line of Control was restored. A statement issued by the Pakistani foreign minister on the pull out issue said it all – Pakistan would appeal to the mujahideen to withdraw, the question of withdrawal of Pakistani forces from the Indian side did not arise as they had not crossed the LOC. This created doubts about the implementation of the plan.

The development of Indian forces in Siachen is also being questioned in the context of the alignment of the LOC. As the LOC terminated at NJ 9842 south of Siachen according to the Simla Agreement, its alignment beyond this point is yet to be determined.

The leaders of various fundamentalist groups who claimed to be fighting in Kargil initially rejected the call of withdrawal with characteristic bravado. Pakistan, as usual, continued to deny that its troops were operating across the LOC. Lately, however, Gen. Musharaf said that some Pakistani troops might have crossed the LOC during aggressive patrolling.

The guerrilla groups operating along with the Pakistan Army in Kargil want the war to go on. According to some of their leaders, "The 10-years old Kashmiri guerrilla war has entered a phase of taking and holding territory as it happened in neighboring Afghanistan against Soviet occupation in the 1980s'. A leader of the Lashkar-e-Taiba boasted that they were making plans to capture more territory elsewhere as they would not be able occupy the Kargil heights during winter.

The comparison of the Afghanistan war with the Kashmir proxy war shows that Pakistan and its surrogates do not understand the nature of the war in Kashmir. Unlike the Soviets, who could not attack Pakistan's heartland, India is quite capable of doing so and also crossing the LOC and capturing vital areas in Pak-controlled Kashmir. India's powerful air force is capable of destroying the Pak logistic support elements and lines of communication leading to Kargil or Siachen. Hopefully, the military capability of the Indian armed forces and the vulnerability of Pakistan and its surrogates have been better understood now by the Pakistani military planners and political leaders.

It must be added that what Pakistan has done has been a great setback for the peace process and the confidence building measures initiated in the recent past. Pakistan seemed to have opted for confrontation and war. Hopefully, it would realise the folly of adopting this option before things spin out of control in South Asia, and lead to events which may threaten the very existence of Pakistan and endanger other countries of the region.

The role of fundamentalists and terrorists in Kargil

Several fundamentalist organisations claim to have sent mujahideen across the Line of Control in Kargil. Actually, only some armed groups from these organisations could have been deployed in support of the Pakistan Army in Kargil sector of Indian Kashmir. Their main role is to sponsor terrorist groups who infiltrate into various parts of Kashmir and commit heinous acts of terrorism, kill political opponents and unarmed minority groups. Brief descriptions of three of the main radical organisations given here may help in understanding their role in Kashmir better.

Lashkar-e-Toiba

On the outskirts of Lahore there is a huge campus. The name 'MARKAZ-E-DAWA-WAL IRSHAD' is emblazoned in bold letters in Arabic script. This is supposed to be a centre of religious education, but it not used to produce highly motivated religious fanatics who join militant organisations such as the Lashkar-e-Taiba (The Army of the Righteous and the Pious often referred to as the Lashkar-e Toiba). Thousands of people assemble here during recruitment rallies. The importance of jihad is drummed in and emotional speeches and rhetoric move people to tears and frenzied chanting. The target of the Indian Army's ruthlessness and the plight of its Kashmiri victims raise tempers and exhort people to settle accounts with the Indians (kafirs).

In this compound, 'Dawa' also runs 30 schools. Here, almost 500 students are given the message of hate and jihad against the 'infidels'. The Lashkar exhorts its members and associates to save their Kashmiri brethren and settle scores with the kafirs (infidels) and their supporters. A 21-day course teaches the essentials of terrorism, assassinations, bomb explosions, improvisation of mines, which can be exploded by remote-controlled devices, and use of a variety of rockets and grenades. Selected students do a specialised course in sabotage and subversion.

Harkat-ul-Ansar

The Harkat-ul-Ansar (HUA) has been renamed 'Harkat-ul-Mujahideen' after it was declared a terrorist organisation by the US government because of its hand in kidnapping and killing foreign tourists in Kashmir.

The objectives of this organisation, however, remain unchanged. Largely mercenaries from Africa, West Asia and some South East Asian countries man it. It is funded by the ISI of Pakistan. The ISI also imparts specialised training and launches these elements for subversion and terrorism into Indian Kashmir and other parts of India.

Hizb-ul-Mujahideen

The Hizb-ul-Mujahideen, the armed wing of the Jamlaat-e-Islami, has a large number of Afghan war veterans in its ranks. Its aim is to 'liberate' Kashmir from India and make it part of Pakistan. It is without doubt a terrorist organisation.

Presently, its task is to spread terror in Indian Kashmir. A part of its programme includes ethno-religious cleansing in the state of Kashmir by either driving out or massacring the Hindus. Its targets are also secular Kashmiri Muslims and the non-cooperative Kashmiris who do not readily provide them shelter or food or propagate their views.

The brand of terror these organisations practise has no sanction in Islam; in fact, killing of the innocent and destruction of public facilitates has been condemned by Islam. The inhuman traits shown by the mercenaries while killing innocent, defenceless Hindus in Kashmir has the stamp of barbaric frenzy and hatred drummed into them in the madrassas of Pakistan. These preachers of hate now have a very large number of supporters in Pakistan. The attire and attitudes displayed in mass gatherings of fundamentalist groups indicate that the fundamentalists of the new generation are not recognizable by their dress or manners. They are not bearded mullahs: they wear jeans and use computers, video cameras and fax machines to spread their message of hate. The Jamaat-e-Islami (JI) organizes periodic gatherings, which are attended by youths from various Muslim countries of Africa and Asia. The JHI indoctrinates them to spread religious fundamentalism, but their motives are political rather than religious. They aspire to capture power. They use Islam merely as a tool to achieve their political ends. Today's fundamentalist is not necessarily a theologian, most are socio-political activists who want to exploit Islam for the purpose of gaining and retaining power.

The Kargil offensive is a manifestation of Islamic resurgence, which was born and bred in Afghanistan with arms aid from the USA and financial assistance from Saudi Arabia. Pakistan is exploiting this situation to its advantage, by using fundamentalists to wage war in Indian Kashmir. The main motive is no longer 'liberation' of Kashmir but to spread a Sunni- Wahabi culture after capturing political power. In the struggle between fundamentalists and moderates (practicing true Islam), the fundamentalists have gained the upper hand both in Afghanistan and Pakistan. A new crop of religious fundamentalists is all set to march into Indian Kashmir.

Violence, which inevitably follows in the wake of fundamentalism, destroys the existing system, but does not build a new one. The barbaric treatment meted out to opponents by the Taliban and massacre of Shias and other minority factions in Pakistan are the signposts of radical Islam. Kashmir must be saved from this variety of fundamentalism.

8

Beyond Kargil

Jaswant Singh

It is now time to look ahead; to look beyond Kargil. But even in charting our course for the future we have to assess what Kargil 1999 was all about? What were the challenges - military and diplomatic? What new facets of our total national commitment and endeavour emerged? What lessons for the years that lie ahead? 'Operation Vijay' - as the Prime Minister said - has resulted in 'Vijay' for India. As we re-examine the military and diplomatic challenges that then confronted us, and which were successfully managed, we need to have a preliminary analysis, draw some conclusions and above all, looking beyond Kargil, draw a route chart for the tomorrows to come.

First, the military dimension. Kargil was a military aggression by Pakistan, with Pak army regulars, across a stretch of the LoC, in four pockets, from the Mushkoh Valley in the west to Tartuk in the Yaldor - Batalik sector in the East. Initially, the element of surprise lay with the aggressor, as is the case with all aggressors. This was soon countered locally. Initially, the terrain, too, conferred some advantage to the aggressor. They had intruded along ridgelines to occupy some key heights and features that dominated a vital road link, between Dras and Kargil. Depth was provided for Pak positions by the ridgelines north of the Pakistan army locations, to provide crucial logistical and administrative support to their troops.

The Indian army's response to the military challenges was measured yet swift, it was focussed, thus effective. The first task was to contain the intrusion. For this an accurate assessment was necessary about the degree and extent of it. This involved amongst other activities the drawing of fire. Simultaneously, a redeployment of troops took place. Through a successful containment of the aggressor's intrusion, the inevitable defeat of this misadventure by Pakistan was ensured. The Indian army through the speed and lethality of its response countered the element of surprise. On 26th May, the Air Force swung into action in support of the group operations.

Out military objective had been clearly spelt out to the intruders - retreat or the Indian army shall evict you. In any event once the intruder's aim of interfering with the Drass-Kargil Highway had been thwarted the whole rationale of this aggression had got defeated. A mere holding of heights was militarily a counter productive venture. They were bound to be evicted - in detail - one by one; for their occupation served scant military purpose. For India, occupation of territory, south of the LoC, was simply not acceptable both physically and as a violation of a principle. Tactical surprise having been lost early by the aggressor, the military principles of superior force, concentration and firepower were bound to tell. And they did decisively. This phase of eviction did not, indeed could not be a phase of battles of manoeuver. The nature of the terrain, the adversary's dispositions plus most importantly our self-imposed restraints about the LoC, precluded those options. The battles for the heights thus became classic infantry actions in high altitude, combining mountaineering and fighting against fixed enemy positions at a higher elevation. They were actions that demanded grit, stamina and dauntless courage. Our troops displayed all these qualities in full measure.

Let us be clear about one other vital aspect. This aggression in Kargil sector was by the Pak regular army, it had the logistic and administrative support of not the Pakistani Army alone but of their total state machinery. Secondly, this misadventure was not aimed at infiltrating into the Srinagar Valley. It was to occupy territory in Kargil and in holding that. This purpose, too, was defeated.

The Kargil aggression is not an extension of the problem of externally aided and abetted cross border terrorism that we have combated until now. It is an overspill of the 'Afghanistan' disorder syndrome'. That is also why it had to be defeated.

In parallel to the military, we also had major diplomatic challenges on our hands. A firm signal had to be conveyed to Pakistan, as also a clear and unambiguous, that in today's age no conflict, least of all one between two nuclear weapons possessing states can escape global media spotlight. This was an additional and a new factor. Managing all these required a qualitatively new level of coordination between the two wings of the South Block - the Ministries of Defence and External Affairs. This too was achieved to demonstrable effect.

Of course, Kargil posed a challenge both to the substance of our foreign policy as also to the conduct of our diplomacy. The Prime Minister had at the very beginning directed the MEA that the true challenge lay in turning back the aggressor, in defeating all his designs, in reversing the aggression but with the maximum of restraint. The MEA had, therefore, also placed before itself the objective of protecting the international flank of the MOD; so that our operations on the ground and in the air could go on unhindered. This was also achieved in no insignificant measure. The first requirement thus was establishing the fact of Pakistan's intrusion and aggression. I would venture to claim that we succeeded in doing so. The next requirement was to spell our objectives with clarity, consistency and candour. This was done early, repeated whenever necessary and can be summed up, sequentially, as the following irreducible minimums. They were:

A) Pakistan's armed intrusion in Kargil will be evicted and its aggression vacated. All Pakistan regular troops and extremist elements under its command and control will have to withdraw. For this purpose, our armed forces will take all necessary action on our side of the Line of Control.

B) Once this intrusion has been cleared, Pakistan would need to reaffirm the inviolability and sanctity of the Line of Control.

C) Dialogue, as part of the Lahore process, which afterall, was initiated by us, could only then be resumed.

Our diplomatic machinery was geared fully to convey these objectives to the international community, as being valid and worthy of support. Continuous interaction was maintained with all the major powers, and the rest of the international community through our diplomatic missions abroad, the diplomatic community in New Delhi and through personal interaction. It is a measure of the justness of India's cause that what I have cited above, as the irreducible minimums, found such a large community of countries standing up in support. Principally, let me repeat, it was because India's stand was recognised as just, thus it was acted upon. I wish to also emphasize that the importance of the inviolability and sanctity of the Line of Control, for maintaining peace and tranquility, was totally accepted by the international community, and Pakistan was held as having violated this Line. Its efforts at terming it as imprecise also failed. Even more, the international community accepted India's view that Pakistan was guilty also of transgressing the territory of trust. The international community also concurred with our assertion that Kargil was a manifestation of this medieval malevolence spilling over from Afghanistan, that these were no freedom fighters, thus there was a need to confront such impulses; in the interest not just of our region but of the larger global community.

It is noteworthy that under the leadership of the Prime Minister, the Ministries of External Affairs and the Ministry of Defence worked as one, the combined synergy of which demonstrated the true power and effectiveness of the Indian State. This is, of course, how it should be. But is is a matter of satisfaction nevertheless, that this was achieved at a time of trial, a time which tests the mettle of any Government's machinery. In this is also a lesson for the future.

There was an added dimension to our total national endeavour. It was the role of our media during Kargil operations. It was marked by exuberant enthusiasm bordering, at times, on the reckless. These young men and women of the media, who were in Kargil, brought the valour of our troops, in the face of great odds, directly into the homes of our citizens. They touched our hearts and eyes with the tales of the bereaved and the families of the fallen. This was our first experience of conflict in the TV/information age. We learnt as we went along. It would be no exaggeration, therefore, to say that the role of the electronic and the print media, in fully informing and mobilizing public opinion, was an invaluable part of the total national effort to meet the challenge of Kargil.

Why did Pakistan undertake such an ill-conceived misadventure? Perhaps, they thought that they could translate the advantage of tactical surprise into a strategic gain by bringing about a defacto realignment of the LoC, in the region, thus rendering the Srinagar-Leh National Highway vulnerable. They were wrong. They miscalculated India's resolve; they did not comprehend the sense of national outrage at this blatant breach of trust, the sheer motivation of the Indian soldiers and the leadership quality of the Indian Army officers who led from the front.

Perhaps, Pakistan calculated on provoking India into escalation. They were wrong again because the decision of not crossing the LoC was taken early and maintained scrupulously, in the face of high casualties and even when the decision to employ air power was taken. The area of conflict was not expanded. Pakistan having disowned its troops as "freedom fighters", could hardly thereafter have opened up a new front, to ease pressure in Kargil.

What of the future? Looking beyond Kargil provides us an opportunity to renew our faith in ourselves, our society, our polity and our nation. It compels us to look ahead in all fields of national endeavour but particularly, in the spheres of national security and foreign policy. One simple message emanating from Kargil is that adequate resources have to be made available for national defence, that the kind of relegation of defence needs that we witnessed in the late eighties and nineties is unsound policy; that technological upgradation cannot be postponed; that the nation must always think of the welfare of those who are in the first rank of its defence.

Kargil has many pointers for our foreign policy and diplomacy too. As in the present instance, we should always be ready to engage with the world as full and responsible members of the international community, but, of course, keeping our national priorities and interests as the guiding principle. We ought to have no reluctance, leave alone fear, in engaging with the world on any issue. Indeed, we serve the national interest when we engage the world on the basis of equality and mutual respect. Such engagement is the very substance of diplomacy. That is not any internationalization of an issue. Nor does it imply mediation or any acceptance of intermediaries.

Issues have to be addressed bilaterally between concerned countries, and in the case of India and Pakistan, that is what the Lahore process is all about. We would like to renew that process and we would like Pakistan to facilitate a resumption of the process, by reaffirming the inviolability and sanctity of the Line of Control. Clearly, a sponsorship of terrorism across the Line of Control, or elsewhere, is a violation of the Line of Control, as indeed of Simla Agreement and Lahore

Declaration. There is a need for Pakistan to abjure sponsoring, aiding or abetting cross-border terrorism. These are not any pre-conditions for dialogue. We are after all, the initiators of this dialogue process and our commitment to it is firm and abiding. But it is only right for our nation, at this juncture, to expect that Pakistan will repair the damage that it has done to trust, that it demonstrates this through concrete and tangible steps. Trust is not built by engaging in dialogue in winter and committing aggression in summer. Continuous calls for Jihad can also hardly be read as messages for dialogue and peace. And it is in this vein that I suggest that high-pitched propaganda against India also does not inspire confidence in Pakistan's interest in dialogue.

I would venture to suggest that Pakistan, too, has to come to terms with its history, as indeed with its geography. It has to realize that there simply is no military solution to what it presumes is its locus-standii in Jammu and Kashmir. It is, of course, for Pakistan to determine its priorities but fomenting religious fundamentalism can hardly be employed, as a tool against want and poverty. India recognizes the permanence of the sovereign state of Pakistan and that is final. While India remains ready for dialogue, the pace at which it can move forward will depend entirely on when and how the state of Pakistan, and what it has now become, permits it to do so.

Our foreign policy has not been fixated on Pakistan, but that has been a significant preoccupation of it. We need to re-examine this in detail. Globally, India has to move purposefully towards realizing its true dimensions- as a major civilisational state, with its own strategic autonomy and strategic space, born out of its economic and political interaction with other countries particularly in the Asia-Pacific community. The real wealth of a nation is its people. History and paucity of appropriate resources prevented us from participating in the economic transformations brought about since the Industrial Revolution. In 1820, Asia contributed 58 per cent of the World GDP; today it is at 37 per cent by 2020, expectations are that it could regain the level of 200 years ago. India has a signal role to play in the coming decades. With our democratic institutions, a large skilled manpower base, geographic location, we must ensure that India rides the crest of this wave.

Through the travail and fire of Kargil our nation has been renewed. The mood though sombre, is confident. National will stands sharpened. The sacrifice of our youth has not and will not be in vain. That is the solemn message of Kargil to the nation and to the world. I close with the poignant words of the memorial at Kohima (Nagaland), that stands tall and proud on a hill, commemorating those who fell in another war:

9

Who is Responsible for Kargil?

Mohan Guruswamy

The campaign to recover the swathe of territory overlooking Kargil from Drass to Batalik occupied by Pakistan is now over. The Indian Army has paid a heavy price to wrest back this area which is as large as the state of Delhi, over a thousand square kilometers, from a determined enemy who has so far fought hard every inch of the way. Even now the army has to beat back attacks and lose lives under constant artillery bombardment. Even if we agree that things turned out well for us, two questions must be answered. Who is responsible for what happened at Kargil? What was the quality of the decision-making and the response of the armed forces?

But first the second. In the euphoria that has followed the eviction of the Pakistanis, we have accepted that the armed forces did well. But did they? The slaughter of our troops in the first fortnight launched in direct assaults against withering fire from well-fortified Pakistani positions speaks volumes of the courage and endurance of the officers and men. Were these the right tactics? The imaginative use of artillery after these initial setbacks and the tactical gain that accrued as a result tell a great deal of the lack of preparedness and confusion in the early stages. Would we have used our men differently if they were mostly drawn from the urban middle and upper classes? Is there a tendency not to value the lives of our jawans, who are mostly from rural and poor families, because somehow they are expendable and because the country cannot make the economic commitment needed to equip the armed forces properly? How effective was the IAF? It seems that the IAF too did not have the tactics and wherewithal to deal with the situation. Was its involvement cost effective? Why didn't the IAF have the tactics and means to cope with mountain warfare? After the Gulf War analysts discovered that the effectiveness of the smart weapons was considerably over-hyped and the reality was quite different. The IAF's performance needs to be put under a microscope. It is the most expensive arm of our defence forces and the nation will want to know if it is getting its money's worth. What was the quality of the operational integration between the two service? It is now the time for some hardheadedness and not to do so would be to invite Kargil's again. Whatever study is conducted must be made public unlike the Henderson Brooks report in the wake of the 1962 debacle that is still a closely guarded secret. What is not so much of a secret is that the report severely castigated the political and military leadership for their failures.

Few seem to realise how close we were to a major debacle when some local shepherds providentially stumbled upon the Pakistani invaders. Given another day or two the Pakistanis would have completely cut-off

Kargil by interdicting the Kargil-Leh stretch of the Srinagar-Leh highway. The Srinagar-Kargil stretch even at best of times is vulnerable to Pakistani artillery. This time they took the heights overlooking the highway and sited direct firing heavy guns completely cutting off Kargil from Srinagar. If the plan had succeeded, Kargil would have been under siege and the brigade headquartered there would have been hard-pressed to hold off the Pakistani Army. With Kargil under siege, Turtuk would have fallen and the Siachen brigades headquarters at Partapur would have been the next target. If the Pakistanis had succeeded, the debacle would have been greater than the fall of Bomdila in 1962. Quite clearly we were taken by surprise and paid a big price for it. Quite clearly someone is responsible for the appalling loss of so many young lives and must be brought to account. It seems that the system is trying to serve up Brig. Surinder Singh, the commander of the Kargil Brigade as a scapegoat. This will not do. The failure goes all the way to the top. Instead of trying to hang an individual we would all be better served if the reasons are analyzed dispassionately and useful lessons derived from them. Harry Truman had a plaque on his table that read: "The Buck Stops Here." The political and military leadership must stop playing passing the buck and get on to accepting responsibility for what happened and giving credit where its due.

The country is outraged by what is perceived as Pakistani treachery carried out stealthily when India's arms of friendship were held out open. Like popular perceptions on these matters usually are, this one too is far off the mark. There is no doubt that this is the perception the government would like the nation to have because that is what serves its immediate interests best. Instead we need to be outraged by the negligence that allowed the Pakistanis to get this far. To continue to feign surprise is to insult the nation's intelligence. The Indian Army too has for long had operational plans in readiness to retrieve the Northern Territories now under Pakistani occupation. An operation to achieve this would inevitably require the crossing of the LOC exactly where the Pakistanis did. The road to Skardu thus must begin at Kargil. If we can plan to move into POK, not to expect the Pakistanis to have a plan to move in the opposite direction would be naïve. The Pakistani operational plan was not a new one. The Pakistani Army first presented it to Benazir Bhutto five years ago. She turned it down deeming it too risky. She was wise. India was in the know of this plan. In fact the Indian Army has been war-gaming this scenario for several years. So what should not have come as a surprise became one because the powers that be were infected with the Lahore fever. Intelligence failure is now being ascribed as the reason, when it is the failure to use one's IQ that is the real cause.

There is much evidence available now to suggest that all the three agencies concerned with intelligence gathering, RAW, IB and DMI, had in-fact provided their masters with ample warning about Pakistani intentions and activities. RAW it seems went as far as telling the government that the Pakistanis were getting ready to launch a major operation in Kargil. It is also now evident that the three responsible political leaders, the Prime Minister, the Defence Minister and the Home Minister, were all warned about what was brewing by their respective snoops. That they did not seem to act is indicative of their naivete, irresponsible attitude or sheer incompetence. The fact that two of the officials directly involved, the then RAW chief and the then Home secretary have been rewarded with cushy post-retirement positions suggests that there might be a quid-pro-quo for silence. Arvind Dave has now become the Governor of Arunachal Pradesh and B.P. Singh has done even better by becoming a Director of the World Bank, just a few weeks after being shunted out as Home secretary. Why? The RAW chief was a double beneficiary of the PMO's largesse having got what many consider an un-merited promotion. Who was his mentor in the PMH? The Subramaniam Committee must find out as to what exactly did the government know and whether they erred in their judgement. There is also much talk that the government knew about the Pakistani occupation of the area by crossing not one, but three ridgelines in some cases, much before the government fell. The suggestion is that it desisted from acting earlier since it wanted to cynically exploit the event for narrow political purposes. The Subramaniam Committee would be doing the nation a great service by either dispelling this or confirming this.

The post Pokhran-Chagai era renders the threat of general war ineffective. A major conventional war runs the risk of escalating into a nuclear conflict and neither India nor Pakistan wants that. The rest of the world will not allow it either. This allows Pakistan a sense of invulnerability that it did not have in Benazir Bhutto's time. The nuclear equation now restricts the two nations to very limited localised conflicts, which can at best be expanded to a short engagement on a larger scale. Thus, if Kargil were to have been besieged, we could have at best made a similar incursion elsewhere to put pressure on the Pakistanis. Ironically enough if that were to have happened it would have been easier for Nawaz Sharif to pull back his forces from the Kargil sector as demanded by the Americans, as it would have led to a similar pull-out by Indian forces.

Now if we had a properly functioning national security analyses apparatus in place instead of an old boys and have-been's club, which the Prime Ministers National Security Council Advisory Board (N-SCAB) now is, this scenario would have been envisaged and appropriate pre-emptive measures taken. The other agency, which could have provided the government with proper inputs, was the Research and Analysis Wing (RAW). But this agency seems under some cloud with known RAW baiters heading the External Affairs and Defence ministries. The Home Minister has also queered things up in RAW by inserting an Intelligence Bureau man as its new head. IB training and experience have little or no relevance to the work RAW does. Reading other peoples mail is only a small part of it. Its real job is to read other peoples minds and analyze the implications of myriad geo-political events such as the fall of Mazar-e-Sharif in Afghanistan and anticipate their implications for India.

It is now known that when the threats emanating from Pakistan were sought to be discussed by the concerned officials with the Prime Minister and his team, they were brushed off as people with old cold war mindsets. In the new post Lahore mood, Vajpayee preferred to be Afzal Khan rather than Shivaji. Vajpayee is reputedly an admirer of Jawaharlal Nehru. There can be no comparison between what happened to Jawaharlal Nehru vis-à-vis the Chinese and what happened to Vajpayee now. Nehru knew what the Chinese were upto but preferred to work things out by engaging the Chinese in talks. Vajpayee did not have a clue about what lay in store at Kargil till it happened.

There is one similarity though. Like in Nehru's time the armed forces have been neglected. Before it came to power, the BJP used to castigate the governments of the day for spending less each year on defence thereby imperiling India's security. In its two budgets it did not reverse this trend. The BJP led government twice turned down a proposal to make a special provision of Rs.2000 crores for indigenous defence equipment over and above the usual defence allocation. The government also failed to undertake a Strategic Defence Review (SDR) as promised in the BJP manifesto. A SDR would have opened its eyes to new risks. Consequently our national security policy did not have any ideas beyond one set of nuclear tests. The lack of clarity on security issues has caused much confusion within the government. For instance after the Pokharan tests L.K.Advani warned Pakistan new geo-political realities and threatened hot pursuit to take out militant bases in POK. Now he swears by the LOC and insists that India will never cross it come what may.

If our security concerns were limited to Pakistan, we did not need to go overtly nuclear. If deterrence is required against all present and future adversaries, the nuclear weapons programme needs to go further. But it is now well known that the Vajpayee government has committed itself to an American administered security regime, which would require India to sign the CTBT and give up the missile programme. While we did not plan for possible post-test scenarios, clearly the Pakistanis have planned well. They have now managed to internationalize the Kashmir issue.

Nawaz Sharif's dramatic dash to Washington, and Clinton's promise to take a personal interest in the matter is an ominous sign. As it is the scuttlebutt has it that our Prime Minister demurred when the US President invited him to join the Clinton-Nawaz talks by saying that with an election imminent a visit now would expose the government to opposition attacks. In any event talks with Pakistan, with some sort of US mediatory involvement will now become inevitable. If that happens Pakistan too would have gained from the conflict.

10

Kargil - The Role of Media

Vijay Naik

Kargil Blunder, for the first time brought into focus the important role played by both the print and the electronic media. It was through their columns and through the little screen that the war reached every home in the country and throughout the world. The role of electronic media was almost restricted during wars India fought against China in 1962; against Pakistan in 1965 and in 1971. The war against China came as a rude shock to Pandit Nehru as while the government and the media were singing the tune of ' Hindi Chini Bhai Bhai' raised during the historic visit of the late Chinese prime minister Chou En-lai, died soon after his visit, as China launched a sudden attack against India, which it was unprepared for such an eventuality. The Indian print media which covered this war extensively brought out many a lacuna in warfare tactics which were latter supported by evidence put forth by the army officers, as one could find in the book 'Himalayan Blunder' by Brig. J.P.Dalvi. In 1999, barely three months after prime miniser Atal Bihari Vajpayee's visit to Lahore, hostilities began in Kargil.

The peace of 28 years between the 1971 war and the kargil war lulled our defence forces into complacency. It was a photo-finish 14 day war which began on the night of December 3, 1971 and resulted in the creadari of Banladesh.The TV was still in its infancy. During the war, correspondents fanned out in the western as well as eastern sectors and reported the events extensively sharing agonies of soldiers and also their joy. The role of Mukti Bahini as a saviour was well brought out by the media. However, what was lost in the fight on the western front (J&K in particular, was compensated with the successes on the eastern front.

One distinction between these wars and the war in Kargil is that while earlier wars were fought on the foreign soil; Kargil war, fought well within the LoC, brought world acclaim for India's agelong sense of tolerance and determination to drive out the enemy from their fortified positions. For the first time in the history of India, which had recently undergone a revolution in the field of telecommunications, we saw an extensive, though selected use of sat-phone which could be hooked from any destination to convey the latest news on the warfront. Earlier, the dispatches of war correspondents were scrutinised by the media officers before they could be sent. But there were no such constraints this time. There was self restraint and dependence on the government machinery.

The electronic warfare in Iraq and its minute to minute coverage by the world media using sophishcated gadgets, however, brought a new sense of confidence among the media that the war could be covered from close quarters of the battlefield, although at ones own risk. The army could not, however, post the correspondents covering war by the side of the soldiers as most of them had to cover it from sanitised areas which were well within the firing range of Pakistan, giving reporters a sense of participation, thrill and danger as one stood near 155 Howitzer Bofors guns which bommed day and night pounding enemy positions entrenched on the treacherous heights of snow capped mountains.TV cameras glued to these guns and the print media could not go much beyond it to report on the actual battle scene, thus making some of the reportage subjective in its content. The war came as a morale booster for the government which had lost majorty in Lok Sabha and was trying to recover from sense of dispair. The partiotic fever created in the country was indeeed an outcome of the success stories, beguiling both the press and the people to believe that there was no intelligence failure on the part of the government. The government maintained that it was not the time to discuss the intelligence failure and their first priority was to drive out the enemy from the Indian soil. The press too put these issues on the back burner untill the hostilities came to an end.

Media's role was generally participatory and supportive of armed forces' actions; though there were differences on how the government was handling the situation diplomatically. It is a fact that what is gained by armed forces in the war is generally lost on diplomatic tables and peace depends on the handiwork of political manoeuvres.

The positive role of media started much before the visit of Mr Vajpayee to Lahore. Needless to say that it was an outcome of an invitation given by Mr Nawaz Sharif through an interveiw to the editor of the Indian Express Mr Shekhar Gupta. Prompt response from Mr Vajpayee resulted in historic bus journey to Lahore in

February 1999. While media in Pakistan and more so in India brought out positive features of this visit which could have become achievements of Vajpayee and Sharif, neither the goverment of India nor the press had any due about machinations of the Pakistan army which had clandestinely put into action the part of 'Operation Topac' plan prepared by the former president General Zia-ul Haq. A personal diary of Lt.Muhammad Maaz Ullah Khan Sumbal of 8 Northern Light Infantry of Pakistan recovered by an Indian army shows that the Pakistani regulars had already moved to much higher peaks along the LoC at same time when Mr Vajpayee and Mr Sharif were busy drafting Lahore Declaration and exchanging pleasantries. On the first page of his diary, Lt Sumble says, " Reached Skardu at 1000 hours and reported to the unit (8 NLI). Capt Mueed Shams Khan was Adjt. Also Capt Sherpur, Capt Imam and Capt Surfraz were there. Maj Raheem and Maj Quzi were CO and 2iC resp. Nice team of offrs." The entry is dated January 2/3 1999. Skardu later came to be known as the most formidable militiary camp of Pakistan in the POK from where supplies of arms and ammunition continued to flow to mujahideens and regulars across the LoC. Print as well as the electronic media gave much hype to Vajpayee's Lahore journey which could have become one of the most important event of this decade, had Kargil war not followed after it. The Indo-Pak war in 1971 lasted only 14 days but Kargil war dragged on for full 53 days taking the toll of army and air force. The severity of the highest mountain warfare was being brought out daily by media which sent young and enthusiastic reporters to the operation theatre spanning the strategic 435 km Srinagar-Leh road, the only link to the Siachen glacier. The Zoji-La pass was known to most of the travellers and Drass was famous for being the second coldest place after Siberia.

Those who went to cover 1971 war in western sector were given military uniforms and ranks to avoid sudden attack on the pressmen during the visit to forward areas. The main briefing was being held in Delhi on daily basis apart from sectoral briefings which were being conducted on the spot by militiary commanders. But during the prolonged action of the IPKF (Indian Peace Keeping Forces) in Sri Lanka or army's action in the Kargil war, none of the pressmen were asked to wear soldier's outfit; is certainly an improvement over 1971. There was comparative freedom in reporting events from the war zone, although daily joint briefings by the spokesmen of army, air force and the ministry of external affairs revealed very little other than what was happening at the actual battle front. A few lucky pressmen and photographers, putting their lives in jeopardy, struggled to get glimpses of action that started in the evening of July 3, 1999 and ended with the capture of the Tiger Hill before the next dawn; passed every detail of valour of our jawans to the respective news headquarters. They were almost 8 kms away from the Tiger Hill and had to depend on the wireless messages received by Commanders at Drass who narrated with caution, some of the details of the fight. The media also put out many heart rending stories of the people who had to leave their everything at the mercy of God; many were hit by splinters and had to lose a limb or two like the injured jawans. It would not be out of place to say that the psychology of the people was 'Kargilised' by regular flow of news. A large number of correspondents covering war could visit war zone only with the help of army which conducted three day tours.

There have been only two incidents of slight injuries to journalists. At Drass, a correspondent was hit by a splinter but was discharged the next day and flown back to New Delhi. The second occasion was when a helicopter carrying a team of journalists taken to see wreckages of Pakistan's reconnaissance aircraft -Atlantis- was targetted by a missile from across the border. Alertness of the pilot avoided disaster.

11

Air Campaign

Air Cmde. N.B. Singh (Retd.)

On May 9, 1999, the Indian Army patrols in Kargil came under fire from Pakistani intruders who had occupied strategic heights close to the vital Srinagar-Leh road on the Indian side of the LOC. Soon after, the Army discovered that the intruders, who numbered about 400, had occupied several hill tops in the Batalik, Drass and Mushkoh sectors of Kargil region. As the situation unfolded, it became clear that the Pakistani Army had carried out a well-planed operation with the following aims. To cut-off Ladakh region from the rest of J&K. The intrusion and occupation of strategic heights in Kargil by Pakistani Army gave an entirely new dimension to Pakistani threat to India in J&K.

The Indian Army which was totally surprised by the Pakistani intrusion in Kargil began operations on May 10 to flush out the infiltrators and dislodge them from their hide-outs on the hill tops.

It was clear that the nature of the intrusion was such that the Army would take time to flush them out and suffer heavy casualties in the process.

Air Power in Joint Operations

On May 25, the Cabinet Committee on Security (CCS) met in New Delhi to consider the situation arising out of Pakistani military intrusion in Kargil. The Chief of the Air Staff, who had earlier visited Kargil was also present at the meeting. After discussion the CCS approved the use of air power and asked the Indian Air Force (IAF) to assist the Army in evicting the intruders from Kargil.

Next day, May 26, the Indian Air Force fighter aircraft and armed helicopters launched air attacks against enemy camps in Mushkoh, Drass, Kaksar and Batalik sub-sectors of Kargil. Over 40 offensive missions were flown from Srinagar and Avantipur air bases located in the Srinagar Valley. MiG-21, MiG-23, MiG-27 fighter aircraft and Mi-17 helicopters were used for air strikes while MiG-29 aircraft provided air cover to the attacking force.

Air strikes against intruders were again mounted on May 27 targeting enemy tented accommodation, logistic stores and suspected hide-outs. There air strikes were jointly planned in consultation with the Army units in the area. From the reports of the local Army commanders, the air attacks were effective and successful. On the same day, the IAF lost two fighter aircraft, a MiG-27 which went down after engine failure, and a MiG-21 which was shot down by a Pakistani surface-to-air missile (SAM).9 The next day, on May 28, the IAF suffered another loss when a Mi-17 helicopter, while on an offensive mission in Drass sector was shot down by a man-portable Stinger SAM fired by the intruders. All 4 crew members, including the two pilots were killed.

Constraints on the use of Air Power

After the first four days of air operations against the intruders in Kargil, it was realised their impact on the ground situation was not very effective due to several constraints, some of them listed below:

1. Though the targets were very close to the LOC, mostly within 5-10 km, the IAF was not permitted to fly over or cross the LOC. This made maneuvering of high speed jet fighters flying at speeds above 1000 km very difficult in a restricted space above the target area.

2. Targets were located at heights of 15,000 feet and above and, therefore, air attacks had to commence from heights above 20,000 feet with disengagement well above the firing range of anti-aircraft ground based weapons and man-portable SAMs like the Stringers, to avoid being hit. This called for flying the aircraft to its limits and needed a high degree of flying skill and aircraft reliability.

3. At heights above 15,000 feet, there was a drop in aircraft and engine performance thus making it more difficult to handle it in attack profiles.

4. Free-fall weapons like rockets and bombs were also affected by lower density and pressure of the atmosphere and therefore, different aiming parameters were required.

5. Locating and identifying targets- small in size- on hill-tops in mountainous terrain was perhaps the most difficult task faced by the IAF.

Air Campaign with New Strategy and Tactics

To counter the problems mentioned above, the IAF urgently reviewed the mission profiles of the previous four days and modified the tactics for air attacks on targets in Kargil and simultaneously inducted Mirage-2000 multi-role jet fighters in the air campaign on May 30. In addition, the air effort on Kargil front was intensified to bring about quick results on the ground.

The induction of Mirage-2000 fighter bombers brought about a qualitative enhancement in the attack capabilities of the IAF which could now perform the following additional tasks.13

1. Effective air strikes could also be launched at night.

2. Precision guided weapons, including laser guided bombs could be used.

3. Deep penetration retarded bombs could be dropped on enemy "Sangars" to penetrate deeply and then blow them up.

4. Electronic warfare systems fitted to the aircraft could be used to jam early warning and missile guidance radars.

In order to intensify operations on the ground also, the Army in Kargil deployed another division which had been moved from the central sector; and the strength of the ground forces in Kargil was now between 30,000 to 35,000 troops. Thereafter, the Army and the Air Force together went on the offensive- the IAF MiGs launching 40 sorties daily to attack enemy positions in Batalik- in which there was intense fighting in the Batalik sub-sector and resulted in the capture of 9 enemy positions by the Army on June 3.15

During the next 20 days, the IAF fighter aircraft were used to soften up the hide-outs of the intruders, their supply lines and supply dumps. Meanwhile, the Army captured a key enemy position in Kargil. On the same day the IAF Mirage-2000 aircraft attacked enemy positions in Mushkoh valley.

The recapture by the Army of a key enemy position in Batalik on June 12 indicated that air and ground operations being conducted against the Pakistani Army intruders were proving successful.

During mid June, the IAF further increased its air effort with intensive air attacks on targets in the north-east of Kargil in an integrated operation with the Army to evict the Pakistani Army intruders from the area. In a major air operation, IAF aircraft launched air strikes on Muntho Dalo camp and targets in Drass and Kaksar. Mirage-2000 aircraft were used in these air raids along with IAF's ground attack aircraft fleet of MiG-21s, MiG-23s, and MiG-27s. Another major objective of these air strikes was to isolate the rest of the J&K from Pakistani intruders. Intensive air strikes were also carried out against targets in Mushkoh valley for this purpose. While these offensive air operations were in progress, the IAF fighter aircraft kept a close watch on Pakistan Air Force F-16 aircraft and helicopters flying on the other side of the LOC and provided a check on violation by them of the Indian airspace.

The IAF aircraft flew a large number of reconnaissance missions to obtain target intelligence and accurately locate enemy concentrations. Films exposed during these missions were processed and thousands of photographs were interpreted by qualified and experienced photo-interpretors at Air HQ, New Delhi, and their report provided, for the first time during the crisis, reliable intelligence about the enemy's location, strength, supply routes and the nature of targets. This greatly assisted the Army and Air Force to effectively plan and conduct joint operations against the intruders. These operations brought in immediate results and there were major gains in Kargil.

The recapture of Strategic heights (Point 4700, Point 5100 and 5000 in Botalik area) by the army was suitobey assistéd by IAF.

The success of the Army in capturing Tiger Hills was made possible by a change in strategy in which the armed forces, infantry, artillery, and the Army Aviation Corps worked in tandem with the IAF. Use of MiG fighter aircraft to bomb bunkers was not very successful till the Mirage-2000 aircraft were pressed into service", an Army officer said. Mirage-2000 aircraft carried out precision bombing of enemy positions and supply routes using laser guided bombs (LCB) and at the same time did valuable reconnaissance missions which provided accurate information on the enemy positions and their supply routes. This information greatly helped the Army in its assault on Tiger Hills.

During the initial phase of the joint Army/Air Force strategy to evict the intruders, the IAF fighter aircraft launched round the clock air attacks against enemy held positions and supply lines which caused immense damage to them and their hide outs. IAF aircraft softened the targets and enabled the infantry to climb up the hill sides without many casualties.

While the air strikes against the intruders in Kargil were launched by the IAF on May 26, the reports indicated that there was a dramatic improvement in the accuracy of attacks only after the induction Mirage-2000 aircraft in operations against the enemy.27

On July 7, while the Army continued to recapture strategic heights in Batalik sector, IAF fighter aircraft struck at a logistic camp west of Tiger Hills as well as attacked targets in Mushkoh Valley. It was reported that the enemy SAMs were encountered during these missions. Later, on July 9, the IAF dropped 40 to 50 tones of bombs on an enemy concentration in Drass sector and demolished a major supply route. The air operations were called off on July 10th.

During a final briefing to the press, the Air Force spokesman summing up the experience gained during the air operations in Kargil said that the air operations had taken place in an environment that was totally new in the history of world military aviation. The IAF had to unlearn what had been taught before as it was operating with a new set of paradigms such as ballistic trajectory of weapons in high altitude operations.

Air Marshal Vinod Patney, Air Officer Commanding-in-Chief Western Air Command, who conducted the air operations in Kargil, summarised the air effort as follows.31

1.	Strike missions	550
2.	Escort missions	500
3.	Reconnaissance missions	150
4.	Helicopter sorties for casualty evacuation and airlift	2185

Impact of Air Operations on Kargil War

The first impact of using air power in Kargil was to make the war multi-dimensional and show the Indian resolve to evict the Pakistani intruders from Indian territory. Further, the use of aircraft by India came as a surprise to Pakistan and upset their plans. Since air power escalated the conflict to a higher level and in another dimension, Pakistan came under pressure from international community to vacate positions held by it in the Indian territory. In addition, the use of air power played and important role in reducing casualties of Indian forces and making the task of evicting the intruders easier.34

Lessons From Kargil Air Operations

The first lesson of the Kargil air operations was the need for adequate intelligence about the enemy intentions and its capability, the type of weapons and the quantities held. Early intelligence, through air reconnaissance, either visual or photographic, would have perhaps, prevented the entire military operation in Kargil. In this instance, intelligence in-puts were needed about the nature of targets and their exact location on maps. This information became available later only after the IAF had flown reconnaissance missions over Kargil.

Adequate advance planning for joint Army/Air Force operations was another important lesson which clearly emerged once again during the Kargil War.

Advance planning for joint ground/air operations are also a must for low intensity conflicts (LIC). In these situations, air power can be effectively used for visual/ photo reconnaissance, quick troops induction, air maintenance, and possible use of armed helicopters.

The air operations in Kargil also indicated the need for planned use of electronic warfare systems to jam enemy early warning and missile guidance radars. In addition, passive jamming devices like chaff and flares would have prevented aircraft losses the IAF suffered during the initial phase of the air campaign by manportable infra-red SAMs. It has clearly emerged that synergised army and air operations and joint mamship gives a major boost is operation.

12

The Intelligence Failure

Major General Y. Bahl (Retd.)

Having studied and analysed the Kargil battle in great detail this part of the book is an attempt to find out why and how this unexpected encounter took us by complete surprise. Which means this is essentially a book about our intelligence machine. While it is certainly not intended to second-guess the Subrahmanyam Inquiry Committee's impending report on the matter, it is quite obvious that our intelligence system failed in Kargil. The Indian intelligence bodies apparently did pick up some warning signals prior to the intrusions and probably anticipated some trouble from across the Line of Control, but they did not quite perceive the magnitude of Pakistan's audacious game plan and thus failed to provide a realistic threat perception to the government.

Having said that, one would like to clarify that the intelligence failure in Kargil does not necessarily mean failure on part of the government. If anything, the government and the country's armed forces must be commended for getting their act together in time and giving a befitting reply to Pakistan's misadventure. Those who criticize the government for the goof-up must realize that whereas our intelligence services have been operating for over 50 years; the BJP led government had just about completed one year at the helm when Kargil happened. And one year was obviously not enough for the government to rectify the fault of the intelligence machine which had been malfunctioning for long, especially for a government that was under tremendous strain of pulls and pressures from within and outside.

In any event, this book does not aim at witch-hunting or pin-pointing responsibility for mistakes committed but it goes beyond the obvious in answering the larger question which is Why did our intelligence fail in Kargil and more importantly – why our intelligence services are, the way they are. It is actually a reminder that unless our intelligence system undergoes a thorough over-haul and works like a well oiled machine, unexpected encounters like Kargil may happen yet again.

THE WAKE-UP CALL

Kargil is not the first incident of a country having been surprised by an unexpected invasion. History is replete with many an episode where lack of intelligence has led to some major military setbacks. The Americans were completely surprised by the Japanese attack on Pearl Harbour. Even Israel was caught unaware by the Arab invasion on the Yom Kippur Day in 1967.

In our own context, even as the nation was celebrating its independence, the Pakistanis surprised us by carrying out a series of raids in Kashmir beginning early September 1947.

While in 1962 we were deceived by China, three years later, it was Pakistan who surprised us again by launching Operation Gibraltar on August 5, '65. A newly raised special task force nicknamed 'Gibraltar Force' comprising regular Pakistan Army soldiers, Militia, Frontier Force Scouts, Razakars and Mujahids with a combined strength of nearly thirty thousand, infiltrated across the cease fire line in civil clothes in two's and three's along selected points between Kargil and Jammu. Some succeeded in penetrating deep into our territory. Since no large-scale infiltration had been predicted by the intelligence agencies, it came as a bolt from the blue for Indian Army. The intelligence failure in Kargil as such, is a case of history repeating itself.

Warning Signals

For execution of any tactical plan, an adversary needs to carry out certain essential activities, which even under utmost secrecy cannot be concealed beyond a certain stage and time. Timely knowledge of these activities reveals the nature and method of conduct of the impending operations. These activities in military parlance are called battle indications. Did Pakistan give out any such indications prior to the Kargil intrusion?

While the exact details of the Pakistan Army's operational plans are still not clear, there were some warning signals, which were some how, overlooked by our intelligence agencies, or so it seems. There were apparently, some major purchases of high altitude military equipment and certain Pakistan Army units on the Line of Control (LOC) in the Kargil Sector were reportedly reinforced through the early spring. According to intelligence sources in Islamabad[1], the Mujahideens strength undergoing training in North East Pakistan, was enhanced significantly towards the end of 1998 and as many as 40 new training camps were established in the Neelam Valley, Muzzaffarabad and Baltistan. The Mujahideens were given intensive training in high altitude warfare by the local mountain guides in the Skardu region by the end of winter. Our own intelligence agency, the Research and Analysis Wing (RAW) reportedly warned of the possibility of a swift, limited Pakistan offensive.

As per the Intelligence Bureau (IB), a report regarding enhanced activity in the Kargil sector was forwarded to the Prime Minister, Home Minister, Cabinet Secretary, Defence Secretary and the Director General Military Operations (DGMO), as early as June'98. The report explicitly warned of Pakistan army regulars building up at various posts and increased fighter aircraft activity in Skardu. The IB also forwarded a report to Home Ministry on December 20'98 regarding intrusion of Pakistani remote-piloted vehicles into the Indian territory at least 20 times.

In March'99, the operatives of Military Intelligence Units, - Intelligence and Field Security Units (IFSU) and Liaison Unit (LU)- based in Leh sent reports about increased threat perception along the border, to the Army Headquarters. Thus all three principle components of the Indian Intelligence machine claim to have given sufficient – if not unambiguous – and timely inputs to the government. Were all these reports and inputs deliberately ignored by the powers that be?

Bunkers or Sangars?

The difference between a bunker and a sangar may not be of much consequence to a civilian but to soldiers – especially Infantrymen – these two types of defences are, in terms of their defence potential and mode of construction, very different. A sangar is essentially a stone walled field fortification erected in a day or two by the defender while taking up a hasty defence. It provides limited protection against small arms and is highly vulnerable to artillery/mortar fire. A bunker on the other hand is a solid defence work made of concrete that provides safety to the defender against small arms, artillery and mortar fire as also adequate cover against air attack. It can take a few weeks to construct a bunker and in a high altitude area like Kargil, may be even a couple of months. There has been a debate whether the Pakistani forces occupying annexed Indian territory in Kargil had constructed Sangars or bunkers as each has a serious implication on the timing of the intrusion. Carrying of stores to make Bunkers at these heights is a Herculean task, which is time consuming and requires a proper infrastructure to accomplish it.

Now imagine the Pakistani intruders carrying out a similar task in our area sans where-withal in winters, with complete secrecy. It's unbelievable. Either our surveillance elements in the area happened to be blind as bats – and deaf as well since construction activity is a noisy affair – or the defences occupied by the intruders were sangars indeed as the army claims.

The Overt Source

Contrary to the popular belief, about 80 % of the information that goes into finished intelligence reports is obtained from open sources such as professional journals, newspapers and other publications. As per IB during the period just prior to the commencement of Operation Vijay in May'99— "Language newspapers in Pakistan and in particular those in Pakistan occupied Kashmir were full of tales of so-called heroic exploits of the Pakistan army and the volunteers in Kargil, Drass and Mushkoh sectors. To assume that our operatives failed to pick up this public information would be stretching things a little to far". The overt sources of information can be exploited only by open minds. We shall further dwell on this later.

The Shepherds Story

It has been reported by a section of the press that it was some local shepherds who informed the army about the presence of Pakistani intruders on our side of LOC. By a strange coincidence, in 1965 too, the first information about the infiltration came from the shepherds. One really wonders, why its is usually the shepherds who give us the wake-up call.

The Tapped Tapes

It is a sad reflection on the psyche of our media, that amidst continuing allegations of intelligence failure, they all but forgot to give a well deserved pat to our intelligencers for their stupendous scoop of wiretapping the conversation between Pakistan Army Chief Gen. Parvez Musharraf (while he was in China) and his Chief of General Staff, Lt. Gen. Mohd Aziz, speaking from Pakistan. We must grant the devils their due. The tapes in question of course have no legal sanctity since in today's hi- tech environment, these can be easily doctored. But, the contents of the taped conversation between the two senior most Pakistan Army officers were very much in consonance with their overall game plan. However, post military coup in Pakistan, the military authorities there have ordered a probe into the leakage of these tapes and have thus added a new dimension to this episode. It is alleged that former ISI chief, Lt. Gen. Ziauddin Butt got the conversation taped and later handed it over to the deposed Prime Minister Nawaz Sharif who sent these to Mr.Vayjapee through Trace II diplomacy. In any event, to get a clearer perspective about Pakistan's sinister game plan in Kargil, let us analyze the following excerpts of conversation, sourced from the Times of India (Internet edition) of

August 7,'99.

" **On shooting down of the Mi-17 helicopter (29 May 1999):**

Lt. Gen. Mohd Aziz (MA): This is Pakistan. Give me room number 83315. Hello.

Gen. Parvez Musharraf (PM): Hello Aziz

MA: The situation on ground is ok... one of their Mi-17 was brought down.

PM: Has this Mi-17 not fallen in our area?

MA: No sir. This has fallen in their area. We have not claimed it. We have got it claimed through the Mujahideen.

PM: Well done.

MA: But topwise side, crashing straight before our eyes.

PM: Very good. Now are they facing any greater difficulty in flying them? Are they scared or not? This also you should note. Are they coming any less nearer?

MA: Yes. There is a lot of pressure on them. They were talking about greater air defence than they had anticipated. They can't afford to lose any more aircraft. There has been less intensity of flying after that.

PM: Very good. First class...

On the line Sartaj Aziz must take and the stand on LoC (29 May).

MA: There is a development. Have you listened to yesterday's news regarding Mian Saheb (Nawaz Sharif) speaking to his counterpart? He said that the spirit of Lahore Declaration has been undone by your people by this escalation and wanted to speak to me thereafter. He told Indian PM that they should have waited instead of upping the ante by using air force and other means. He [Sharif] told him[Indian PM] that Sartaj Aziz could go to New Delhi to explore the possibility of defusing tension.

PM: OK.

MA: Which is likely to take place, most probably tomorrow.

PM: OK.

MA: Our other friend (Lt. Gen.Ziauddin, director general ISI? Or could it be United States) might have also put pressure. For that, they will have a discussion at foreign office about 9.30 am today and Zafar saheb (Lt. Gen. Saeeduz Zaman Zafar, acting Pakistani army chief and commander 11 Corps) is supposed to attend.

PM: OK.

MA: Aziz Saheb (Sartaj Aziz) has discussed with me and my recommendation is that dialogue option is always open. But in their first meeting, they must give no understanding or commitment on ground situation.

PM: Very correct. You or Mehmood (Commander X Corps, Rawalpindi) must go with Zafar because they don't know about ground situation.

MA: This week we are getting together. Zafar saheb will deliberate on it. We want to suggest to Zafar that they have to maintain that they will not be talking about ground situation.

PM: Idea on LoC?

MA: Hint is that, given that the LoC has many areas where the interpretation of either side is not what the other side believes. So comprehensive deliberation is required. So that can be worked out by the DGMOs (director general military operations).

PM: They have to assure that we have been here from a long period. Like in the beginning, the matter is the same – no post was attacked and no post was captured. The situation is that we are along our defensive Line of Control (LoC). If it is not in his (Sartaj Aziz's) knowledge, then discuss it altogether. Emphasize that for years, we are here only. Yes, this point should be raised. We are sitting on the same LoC since a long period.

MA: This is their (India's) weakness. They have not agreed on the demarcation under UN's verification, whereas we have. We want to exploit it.

PM: This is in Shimla Agreement that we cannot go for the UN intervention.

MA: Our neighbor does not accept their presence or UNMOGIP arrangement for survey of the area. So we can start from the top, from NJ 9842. On this line, we can give them logic but in short, the recommendation from Sartaj Aziz saheb is that he should make no commitment in the first meeting on military situation. And he should not even accept cease-fire, because if there is cease-fire, then vehicles will be moving (on

Drass-Kargil highway). In this regard, they have to use their own arguments. We don't know but there is no justification about tension on LoC. No justification. We want to give them this type so that he does not give any specifics. If there is more critical situation, then the visit should be deferred for another day or two....

Nawaz Sharif's ignorance and Pakistani army control over terrorists in Kashmir (26 May)

MA to PM: But he (unidentified senior person) was also saying that any escalation after that should be regulated as there may be danger of war. On this logic we gave the suggestion that there was no such fear as the scruff of their (militants) neck is in our hands, What ever we want we could regulate it.... We told him (Nawaz Sharif) that there is no reason of alarm and panic.

Then he said that that he came to know of it seven days back, when corps commanders were told. The entire reason for the success of this operation was total secrecy. Our experience was that our earlier efforts failed because of secrecy problems. So, the top priority is to accord confidentiality, to ensure our success. We should respect this and the advantage we have from this would give us a handle.

Even a casual study of the above conversation makes it quite obvious that:

Pakistan regular army personnel had been fighting alongside mujahideens from the very beginning

One of their main objectives was to alter the LOC to their advantage.

The Indian Air Force (IAF) MI-17 helicopter was fired at on the Indian side of LOC.

They did not want the operation to escalate into a full-fledged war.

Pakistan Army had full control over the militants activities

And, there is inadequate control of the civilian government over the army generals.

THE INTRUDERS

If you know the enemy and know yourself, you need not fear the result of a hundred battles. If you know yourself but not the enemy, for every victory gained you will suffer defeat. If you know neither the enemy nor yourself, you will succumb in every battle. These are the words of ancient Chinese philosopher Sun Tzu. We know our capabilities and ourselves quite well. But how much did we know about the enemy, in the initial stages of the conflict?

Groping in the Dark

The first signs of intrusion were detected on 4/5 May'99. But it was only after about 10 days, that the extent of the intrusion became somewhat clear. Well, it will not be fair to blame the Army for taking its own time to assess the ground reality. A proper review of the situation, especially in an unconventional scenario such as the Kargil invasion, takes time. The attacking force must get a fair estimate of the enemy strength, dispositions and capabilities before mounting the offensive. This is usually done by launching patrols or even probing attacks – and that's what our army did. Two patrols were dispatched on May 4/5, one to Khoberaro and another to Yaldor. The first patrol saw two men while the second patrol observed seven intruders. Two officer led patrols were launched the next day. However both were ambushed and three soldiers were killed.

Narrating the sequence of events thereafter to the press, Lt. Gen. Krishna Pal, GOC 15 Corps said, " By then, it became clear we needed extra troops. We took a two pronged action and moved 1 Naga and 8 Sikh from the Valley on May 11 and 13 respectively. The GOC of 3 (Infantry) Division at Leh simultaneously moved two battalions - 1/11 Gorkha Rifles and 12 J&K LI which were on their way down from Siachen. Since these battalions were acclimatized, they were effective in containing the enemy from reaching the Indus Valley. The Naga and Sikh battalions which were not acclimatized took up blocking positions at heights of 16,000 – 18,000 feet at Drass".

The Invading Force

As per the initial estimates the number of Pakistani intruders was put at around 300 mujahideens which was later enhanced to 700 mujahideens reinforced by Pakistan Army regulars. Later the strength of the Pakistani invading force was estimated to over 1000 (mainly Pakistan regulars assisted by mujahideens) consisting of the following:

· Units of Northern Light Infantry comprising troops of the northern areas of Pakistan.

· Mercenaries of the Harkat -ul-Mujahideen (HUM). The group was known as Harkat – ul – Ansar before it was banned by the US after it abducted foreign tourists (including US citizens) in Kashmir Its cadre comprising nearly 80 percent foreign mercenaries who had been trained in Osama Bin Laden's camps in Afghanistan.

Lashkar-e-Toiba, a well trained and heavily armed militant group formed in the early 1980's is currently the ISI's favourite. Fighting the Ghazwa-e-Hind - holy war against India – the group with mostly militants from Afghanistan and Pakistan occupied Kashmir (POK) on its rolls, also claims to have links with Bin Laden.

· Al Badr, formed in 1998, comprises elements of the dreaded militant organization Hizbul Mujahideens from both POK and J&K. Its training camps are located in POK.

· Osama Bin Laden's Harzat-ul-Jihad-al-Islami , also known Tehrik-e-Jihad and Al Qaeda.

World's most wanted terrorist: Osama Bin Laden, son of a Saudi Arabian construction millionaire and one of the FBIs (Federal Bureau of Investigation) ten most wanted fugitives, is believed to have called for an all out jehad against India. In his threat that appeared in the September 16 issue of Jang – a popular Urdu daily published in Pakistan –Bin Laden declared: "... all mujahadeen groups in Pakistan should come together now to target India... we are always ready to help the Kashmir mujahideens"[7].

During the Kargil conflict, there were rumours of the presence of Bin Laden and his mercenaries in the battle zone. While the individual presence of the world's most wanted terrorist could not be established, there is little doubt about the presence of his followers in Kargil.

THE BLAME GAME

Soon after the culmination of the Operation Vijay, the government ordered an inquiry into events that led to the Pakistan's intrusion in Kargil. But even as the inquiry committee was trying to find out the truth of the matter, the political parties went full lick to derive political mileage during election time out of this sorry affair. There have been charges and counter-charges. Worse, even the armed forces have not been spared in this blame game.

THE INTELLIGENCE MACHINE

Why our intelligence failed in Kargil? A straight question, though sans a straight answer. A section of the press seems to have delved into the issue and in consultation with some of our prominent defence analysts has tried to address this question. But, perhaps due to the inherent constraints of time and space that the newspapers and periodicals face, most lead articles and cover stories published so far, have only scratched the crust of the matter, leaving the core untouched.

While some have blamed the lack of intelligence culture which is supposedly deep rooted in India's history, others have out rightly criticized our intelligence agencies for being negligent and unprofessional. Lack of hi-tech surveillance equipment has also been cited as one of the reasons for the failure of our intelligence machine.

Agreed, there is an element of truth in all these allegations, but the real malaise lies much deeper. For a comprehensive answer to this question and to get a deep insight into this burning issue, we must first critically analyse our existing intelligence setup and find out why our intelligence agencies are, the way they are. It will also be in the fitness of things to compare the organization and functioning of CIA and ISI with our own outfits. CIA, because it happens to be the world's most powerful secret service and ISI, being the sole intelligence agency in Pakistan and deals with the dirty tricks for our main adversary. Besides, both have been active - at times, jointly – in India.

Historical

The aim is not to trace the history of our intelligence services and to provide an element of continuity to the entire analysis. In addition, also point out as to how deep-rooted is the intelligence culture in India's history.

"As the wind moves everywhere and penetrates all created beings, so also should the king penetrate everywhere by means of his unidentified agents." Thus advised Manu, the mythological lawmaker. Kautilya, considered as the master of espionage in ancient India, lays out an effective system of espionage in his 'Arthasastra', the manual of statecraft. Espionage, both diplomatic and military was highly organized. Kautilya describes how spies were used to investigate enemy positions and numbers. He also mentions the sending back of messages in cipher by carrier pigeons, demoralizing the enemy by circulating false information and attempting to seduce allegiance of important individuals in the army and the harems. The Rigvedas also mention of 'dutas' and 'prahitas'. While the former was a diplomatic envoy of the king the latter was supposed to be a regular spy. Even the great Indian epics, Mahabharata and Ramanayana explicitly mention the activity of secret agents. The art of spying was an important facet of good governance and as such spies were extensively employed by the kings, as is evident throughout our recorded history up to the Mughal period. Thus, espionage in India is as old as the origin of the state.

Moving on through the times, it was during the British rule in India that our present intelligence setup was conceived and formalised. The first agency responsible for collecting intelligence on internal security was called the Anti Thugee organization which was established by the British in 1935. However, one of our main intelligence agencies which exists today – the IB – was an offshoot of Police Department (CID) and came into existence much later in 1929, after undergoing a series of organizational and functional changes. Post independence, IB continued to be the sole agency responsible for both internal as well as external intelligence till September 1968, when RAW was created to look after the foreign affairs. Military intelligence service – the MI – based at Shimla was in existence throughout the British rule, however its main component, the Intelligence Corps was instituted in 1942 and was headquartered at Karachi.

The Intelligence Services

There are generally two types of intelligence services which gather and evaluate information for the country's political and military leaders to help them in decision making during peace and in war. One gathers and analyses information, which is processed and analyzed and then becomes intelligence.

In India there are several agencies which carry out both the tasks. Mainly the IB is responsible for providing intelligence for the country's internal security and RAW looks after the external intelligence. The third component of our intelligence machine is the Military

Intelligence that is dedicated to all the three defence services. Besides, some para military forces like Border Security Force (BSF) have their own intelligence units called the "G" branch. There are others such as Directorate of Revenue Intelligence, the Narcotics Control Bureau, CBI and CID. These form an essential part of the entire intelligence setup but are not being discussed here since they have very little to do with the Kargil episode.

At the top of the intelligence hierarchy is the PMO (Prime Ministers Office) and the Cabinet Committee for Security Affairs (CCSA), followed by the Cabinet Secretariat. The highest intelligence assessment body, the Joint Intelligence Committee (JIC), comprising representatives of all the intelligence services, forms part of the National Security Council's secretariat. Its task is to coordinate all intelligence related activity viz. Political, economic, scientific and military and prepared weekly reviews and special reports, as required by the Prime Minister, the Cabinet, various ministries and government departments.

INTELLIGENCE BUREAU

The Organization

The IB is essentially a counter-intelligence organization controlled by the Union Home Minister, which deals with all intelligence matters pertaining to India's internal security. It is divided into various headquarters and field units based on its specific functions such as security, insurgency and immigration etc. The Director IB is the country's highest ranking police officer and a member of the JIC. Right since its inception, IB has been a police oriented organisation and as such, not only its top boss but also its main officer cadre is recruited from the Indian Police Service. Its technical manpower is inducted through Union Public Service Commission or directly from the universities.

The Track Record

Tribal Invasion of Kashmir – Soon after the partition, the newly formed and belligerent Pakistan launched the tribal invasion of Kashmir in September'47. The IB, despite its teething problems and limited resources, did provide some useful inputs regarding Pakistani intentions in Kashmir, based on which India could take the Pakistan challenge head on.

The Chinese Aggression – Even though the IB had failed to report the construction of the strategic road across Aksai Chin by the Chinese in the early 50's, it had apparently provided sufficient and timely information to the government regarding Chinese threat before the actual invasion in 1962.

However, the bits and pieces of information gathered by the IB remained more or less like a jigsaw puzzle, since the same was not processed into hardcore intelligence. Nehru's misguided policy on China did not help matters either. The Chinese attack was not unexpected as such, but they surprised us all the same because we had our blinkers on.

Indo-Pak War 1965 – Three years after the '62 debacle we had still not completely woken up it seems. Not only were we taken aback by Pakistan's 'Gibralter Force', our assessment of their Grand Slam, was also not up to the mark. The IB claimed that it had provided adequate intelligence about Pakistan's grand design but the same was not properly interpreted by the end users.

If we accept the IB's claim as correct and not a mere face saving device, then the Indian Army must be blamed for its faulty assessment of the available intelligence. But then, was it intelligence or mere pieces of unprocessed information that were dished out by the IB?

Counter-Insurgency Operations – India has been facing the menace of insurgency since the fifties. It started in the North- East and has now spread almost through out the country. IB painstakingly established its network in all the insurgency prone areas and had several successes to its credit in providing hard intelligence during counter-insurgency operations. However, it has failed miserably on some occasions resulting in serious setback to the end user, mainly the army. Operation Blue Star is one such instance. The experience in counter insurgency operations in Doda has been no different. When the elite Delta Force (Rashtriya Rifles) was inducted into the Doda District in 1994, as part of the counter insurgency grid in J&K, real time information from the existing IB sources was hard to come by.

Communal Riots – Ever since the time of partition when we witnessed the worst riots between the Hindus and Muslims, communal disturbances have become a recurring feature in this country. Out break of communal violence, of course is difficult to predict, but then, isn't the job of our intelligence agencies to predict the unexpected. Acquisition of real time intelligence in such a scenario has to be an ongoing process, which the IB has not been able to follow, or so it seems. In recent times, IB's inability to anticipate the aftermath of Bombay blasts, had been a major failure on its part.

RESEARCH & ANALYSIS WING (RAW)

RAW was created in September 1968 as an offshoot of the IB – its foreign intelligence desk and the Directorate General of Security (DGS) are a legacy of the IB – and was placed under the control of Cabinet Secretariat. It is responsible for collecting, analyzing and disseminating intelligence, particularly external intelligence, which has an effect on our national security. A Director, an officer of the rank of a secretary, heads it.

The Track Record

RAW has been active both within and outside India for almost three decades but its track record like the IB is a mixed bag. Within two years since its inception it performed stupendously alongside the Mukti Bahini for liberation of Bangladesh. However its attempt to do a Bangladesh in Sri Lanka in the mid 80's boomeranged on the IPKF (Indian Peace Keeping Force). But to be fair it is actually the political leadership that must be blamed for the Sri Lanka fiasco. On the insurgency front, especially in Punjab during Operation Blue Star and the J&K thereafter, RAW has been off the target more often than not.

Military Intelligence

The organisation

Technically, Military Intelligence (MI) covers the intelligence setup of all three defence services, however its army component being the largest and most prominent, the term is commonly used with reference to the army intelligence. At the apex of the organization is the Directorate General of Military Intelligence (DGMI) which is headed by a Lt.Gen and functions under the Vice Chief of Army Staff. Similarly, there are directorates of air and naval intelligence functioning under their respective headquarters in New Delhi. It was primarily the army's Intelligence Corps (Int Corps) that had an active role to play in Kargil, as such its organization alone is being highlighted here.

The DGMI controls and coordinates the overall intelligence activities of the army and comprises of various country and function specific desks. Its main intelligence apparatus – the Intelligence Corps is divided into two parts – the LU and IFSU. While the former is responsible for counter intelligence, the latter acquires external intelligence for the army. Both the units are manned by volunteer army officers and other ranks that are permanently seconded to the organizations after undergoing specialized training at the Military Intelligence School in Pune.

The Track Record

The MI too has not been very consistent in delivering the goods and its record of achievements is interlaced with failures like that of other two intelligence agencies. Whereas it performed admirably during the 1971 operations, its efficiency during the Chinese aggression in 1962 and Pakistan's offensives in 1948 and 1965 was far from satisfactory. However, it has played an important role in some of the major counter insurgency operations undertaken by the army as enumerated below:

Operations in the North – East – The Indian Army has been combating intelligence in the North East for several decades. But it was only in the 90's that it intensified its operations to counter the growing menace of insurgency, especially in Assam. Operation Bajrang, Operation CloudBurst and Operation Rhino were launched in succession, commencing towards the end of 1990. During Operation Rhino, the Int Corps was well prepared and had acquired substantial information about the ULFA operatives which contributed to the success of the operation.

Operation Pawan – The MI apparently did not quite anticipate the government's rash and sudden decision to send IPKF to Sri Lanka and as such was caught off guard during the initial stage of Operation Pawan. But why RAW, which had been training LTTE cadres all along, could not – or rather did not - provide any worthwhile information to the Indian Army, is something of a mystery that one has not been able to unravel. Anyway, the army got down to business with locally acquired tourist maps and the MI, even though late off the starting blocks, got its act together and played a vital role in IPKF's operations by providing hard intelligence – mainly acquired through Signal Intelligence (SIGINT) – to the army units.

Operation Rakshak. One of the major achievements of MI has been the intelligence acquisition during Operation Rakshak, both in Punjab as well as in J&K. Despite its perennial problem of coordinating the intelligence effort with other agencies, the Int Corps was able to build its own network in both the States, especially the latter – a fact which is manifested in many a successful operation executed by the army units employed in Operation Rakshak.

INTER SERVICES INTELLIGENCE

With the advent of terrorism in Punjab and J&K, as also thanks to the media blitz, the average Indian who perhaps may not have ever heard of RAW or IB, is now quite aware of Pakistan's ISI. The hand of ISI is seen in all the troubles from Kashmir to Kanyakumari and Kutch to Kohima. However, the larger than life image that ISI seems to enjoy in India is partially because of its own abilities and mostly because of our own failure to effectively counter its growing menace.

The Organization

The organizational structure of ISI is quite similar to most other intelligence agencies in the world but the absolute power it enjoys in Pakistan is something that even the omnipotent KGB could never boast of.

The ISI is headed by a Director General (DG) of the rank of Lt Gen/Maj Gen, who is invariably a serving officer of the Pakistan Army. The ISI being an inter-services organization, its DG can be from any one of the three services but ever since its inception this elite outfit has never been headed by an officer from Pakistan Airforce or Navy, the reason being that the DG is always the Army Chief's man, even though on paper he functions under the Ministry of Defence and is supposed to be the adviser to the Prime Minister on intelligence matters.

The ISI is broadly structured as follows:

The Joint Intelligence Bureau (JIB) – This is the largest bureau of the ISI having three sections/sub-sections including one dealing specifically with India. The JIB is not only responsible for posting and functioning of Pakistani Defence Attaches/Advisers to foreign countries but also controls the movement of foreign defence attaches within Pakistan.

· **The Joint Counter Intelligence Bureau (JCIB)** – This bureau is responsible for surveillance of foreign suspects as also the political leaders, civil servants, police and armed forces of Pakistan. Such misuse of intelligence services is quite common in other countries also. In fact, our own IB, is known to keep tabs on senior defence services officers among others. However, while IB carries out such surveillance at the behest of the central government, the ISI does so on behalf of the Pakistan Army.

· **Joint Intelligence Miscellaneous (JIM)** - It is responsible for espionage activities in other countries and is perhaps the most destructive component of the ISI. The JIM carries out assigned tasks either through its own agents or through officers posted in cover appointments in Pakistani missions abroad. Trained spies are also sent to carry out offensive --read destructive – intelligence assignments in the target countries. While members of the JIM are known to have crossed international borders to keep in touch with their agents, most activities on and across the borders are controlled by the army's Field Intelligence Units.

· **Joint Intelligence North (JIN)** – This is a Kashmir specific bureau that along with the JIM is presumably the hub center of all ISI activities in J&K.

· **Joint Signals Intelligence Bureau (JSIB)** – As its name suggests the bureau carries out SIGINT activities for the ISI.

· **Joint Intelligence Technical (JIT)** – This bureau functions alongside other bureaus – especially JSIB – and advises ISI on technical aspects of counter intelligence.

Joint Intelligence Administration (JIA) This bureau provides the administrative back up to the ISI and its personnel posted abroad.

The ISI can be compared to a combination of the RAW, IB, CBI, various special agencies operating under the Indian Home Ministry, the intelligence directorates of our armed forces and para-military forces and the JIC, all rolled into one. It is the sole and ultimate intelligence machine piloted through remote control or otherwise by the Pakistan Army Chief himself.

The Track Record.

Considering its overall scheme of things, the ISI's track record needs to be judged essentially on three fronts i.e. on home turf inside Pakistan, in Afghanistan and most significantly inside India. On the home front, the ISI's role in toppling successive leaders from Zulfiqar Ali Bhutto to Nawaz Sharif – barring Gen Zia-ul-Haq – is too well known to be repeated here. Outside it has always been actively operating in Afghanistan, especially since the entry of the Russians in Afghanistan ten years back. It performed admirably alongside CIA and is largely – and rightly - credited for its efforts in evicting the communist regime and the Russians from Afghanistan. However, it is India, where the ISI has been most active of late. In fact, it has successfully managed to divert some of its efforts and weapons as also those of the Mujahideen's – from Afghanistan to J&K. The Pakistan sponsored terrorism in India is actually a repeat of its Afghanistan strategy, wherein Pakistan regulars and the Mujahideens are operating as a single entity. The ISI could not really succeed in exploiting the Punjab problem and had to cut a sorry figure as despite all its support to the Punjab militants, the militancy was successfully curbed by the Indian security forces. Its efforts to ferment trouble in the North East States of Nagaland, Mizoram and Assam have also not produced the results desired by Pakistan. However, in J&K, the ISI has enjoyed a series of successes and post Kargil, it has intensified its efforts towards achieving the ultimate ambition of Pakistan, that is to wrest Kashmir.

WHAT AILS OUR INTELLIGENCE MACHINE?

After having had a look at the organizational structure and track record of our principal intelligence services, one needs to delve into the next logical question: what exactly ails our intelligence machine and why it malfunctioned in Kargil?

Even a cursory glance at the events as they unfolded in Kargil will suggest that it was not one particular component of the intelligence machine that failed to function properly but it was a systemic failure in general that did us in.

The Subrahmanyam Inquiry committee instituted by the Central Government on the Kargil conflict is expected to submit its report soon and it is not to second guess the inquiry commission's report nor is it possible to do so. The commission may pinpoint the faults but not the defaulters, and rightly so. After all, there has been a systems failure and as such the whole machine needs a thorough over-haul. Rolling down a few heads is not really going to improve matters, at least not in the long run. It would therefore be in the fitness of things to look for the Achilles' heels in our intelligence system, and turn them into Samson's hair, rather than indulge in the futile blame game and witch-hunting.

The Organisational Structure - From a mere study of organization of our intelligence agencies, their basic structure appears to be more or less similar to other such organizations the world over. The problem seems to be at the top, that is the JIC, which like a toothless tiger lacks the regulatory authority and as such is not given due importance by the agencies functioning under it. The intelligence services often do not share the information among each other and if that is not bad enough, they also tend to directly access the powers that be, thus bypassing the JIC whose quintessential role is to coordinate and assess the entire intelligence effort. Their main rival, the ISI being the sole agency that collects, collates and converts information from all the available sources into intelligence, faces no such problem of coordination.

Another aspect connected with the organization of our intelligence services that needs to be looked into is the autonomy enjoyed by them. While it is essential that such organizations must be given sufficient freedom to operate independently without undue government interference, for obvious reasons they can not be allowed to build their independent empires free from any public scrutiny. It may therefore be worthwhile, to emulate the CIA model in this regard. The CIA even though being an independent agency is accountable to the American people through the US Congress Intelligence Oversight Committee.

Politicization -Politicization of any government organization is bad for the system; politicization of intelligence services is even worse, especially in a democratic country like India. It not only curbs the initiative and independent functioning of an organization but also leads to various other ills such as political vendetta and misuse of power for political gains. There have been a few occasions when services of covert units of RAW have been utilized to destabilize certain state governments considered inimical to the political interests of the ruling party at the center.

At the time of its inception, RAW would have been placed under the Ministry of Defence but for Mrs.Indira Gandhi who realized the value – read political benefit – of having such an organization under the Cabinet Secretariat P.N.Haskar, her Principal Private Secretary at that time, backed her up and thus RAW was instituted under the Cabinet Secretariat. If it was Haskar who was instrumental in placing RAW under direct control of the Cabinet Secretariat, it was R.N.Kao who enjoyed maximum power as RAW's Chief during Mrs. Gandhi's tenure as Prime Minister. And even as RAW and Kao both became extremely pervasive and powerful when Mrs.Gandhi was at the helm, the IB was placed under the oversight control of the Policy Planning Cell, then headed by P.N.Dhar. By a strange coincidence as it were – or was it by design? – Haskar, Kao and Dhar, all three belonged to the Kashmiri pundit clan of Mrs.Gandhi. Needless to say, personal equations between political leaders and intelligence chiefs are not in organizational interest and in fact prove counter productive for both and should be avoided as such.

Coordination - The intelligence failure in Kargil could be largely attributed to lack of coordination between various agencies operating in the area viz. the Int Corps, RAW, IB,CID and the Indo-Tibetan Border Police (ITBP). Even though they are often located close by, the coordination is missing and they end up reporting along their respective chains of command. By the time the information trickles in down the line, it is often of no use.

While lack of coordination dissipates the over all intelligence effort, over lapping of functional roles of certain agencies results in duplication of their work. A case in point is the covert outfits functioning under the Cabinet Secretariat – SSB and SFF – who seem to be duplicating the work of BSF and ITBP, the two border forces under the Ministry of Home Affairs. A three member review committee under former home secretary K Padmanabhaiah, set up by the government to look into the functioning of these super secret services has reportedly recommended disbandment of SSB and absorption of its personnel in other intelligence agencies. However, it is doubtful if the proposed disbandment will take place, since the affected personnel are apparently lobbying hard for maintenance of status quo as they apprehend loss of their seniority if they are side stepped to other agencies.

One - upmanship – One of the main reasons for lack of coordination of intelligence effort is the element of one-upmanship that exists amongst various agencies. Whereas healthy competition acts as a source of inspiration for any organization, unhealthy professional rivalry wherein one tries to score a point over the other can be counter productive. But unfortunately this happens quite often.

Professionalism – When Elvis Presley, the most famous American pop icon of his time was summoned for his tour of duty by the US Army, he drove to the nearest military headquarters in his chauffeur driven Rolls Royce, but left the car outside the headquarter gates and walked inside the premises like a common US citizen with a duffel bag slung over his shoulder. This was perhaps a symbolic gesture on his part signifying that he had left his normal life style and attitude behind and was all set to take on the rigours of military service. He was a thorough professional and meant business as a pop star and as a soldier. The officers seconded to the intelligence corps needs to be very motivated and have a professional attitude.

It is not only the Int Corps that is lacking in professionalism. The other agencies are no different and since this seems to be our national weakness. With the recent economic liberalization, our private sector has been forced to adopt virtues of professionalism by the multi national companies. It is time our intelligence set up follows suit.

Foresight – To be successful in its missions, an intelligence organization must be able to predict the unexpected. For this, besides the professional acumen, one needs to think ahead with foresight. Unfortunately, like professionalism, the sense of foresight - or rather lack of it – too happens to be our national weakness and is visible everywhere. Lack of adequate basic infrastructure, unplanned cities with heavily congested roads and choked drainage system, absence of effective disaster management plans, population explosion with all its connected problems, lopsided health and education policies – the list is endless – are all due to lack of foresight on part of our political leadership and bureaucracy.

Our intelligence system obviously is no different. Some of the intelligence failures discussed earlier are attributable to lack of foresight, above all else. The fiascos of Operation Bluestar and Operation Pawan were actually quite predictable had the persons concerned bothered to look ahead. During Bluestar, why was it that the troops of only a few army units resorted to mutiny whereas other units having same class composition of troops, remained unaffected? The reason is simple – the commanding officers with foresight could anticipate the trouble and had motivated their men accordingly. Those who did not predict the unexpected were caught unaware by the pitfall.

Acceptance of Intelligence – As brought out earlier, some political parties have out rightly blamed the government for Kargil intrusion and in fact pronounced it guilty of deliberately ignoring vital information provided by the intelligence agencies about Pakistan game plan well in time. Some opponents of Mr.Vajpayee have gone to the extent of blaming him personally for willfully ignoring the intelligence reports, as acceptance of same would have jeopardized his Lahore bus initiative. While these allegations of course are far fetched and without any substance, there have been occasions in the past when hard intelligence was not accepted by the leaders, perhaps due to their political compulsions. For instance in 1975, the then IB Chief, Mr. Jayaram had advised the Prime Minister against promulgation of emergency but Mrs. Gandhi did not accept his advise as it was contrary to her political ambition and went on to impose emergency on the country and thus blemished the otherwise spotless image of India as the world's largest democracy.

Similarly, Mr.Rajiv Gandhi chose to ignore repeated warnings from the intelligence agencies regarding clear threats to his life but he probably did not want to lose his mass appeal and thus continued to mingle with the crowds at his own peril.

Needless to say, the best intelligence is of no value unless it is accepted by the decision maker, but unfortunately an unbiased objective analysis provided by the intelligence apparatus quite often finds no takers at the decision making level. As such, in order to please their political bosses, the intelligence heads sometimes modify their intelligence inputs instead of acquainting the decision-maker with unvarnished bitter truth.

Consistency – No organization can be expected to have a cent percent success rate and capability to deliver goods unfailingly all the time, least of all the intelligence machine. Because more often than not, the intelligence analysts are required to grope in the dark, deals with intangibles and still make fairly accurate predictions. To add to their woes, many ambiguous situations and conflicting indicators are all part of the intelligence puzzle. And then the adversary obviously is not obliged to follow the pattern as may have been projected by the analysts after carefully and diligently processing all available inputs. Not surprisingly therefore, track record of all intelligence agencies including the highly rated CIA and ISI is a mixed bag. Even thoroughly professional outfits such as Mossad and the KGB have sometimes gone completely off the target in their intelligence assignments.

In Kargil our intelligence machine did pick up bits and pieces of information but somehow failed to solve the complete jig saw puzzle. Whatever they may say now, our intelligence pundits could not provide an unambiguous, accurate and timely assessment of the Pakistan designs in Kargil to the government. They did anticipate some problem but could not perceive the magnitude of the Pakistan's efforts in the sector. Their threat perception at best was an underestimated one and therefore may have been underrated by the people at the helm. But let us face the fact. It is not the first time nor will it be the last that our intelligence machine became dysfunctional. As long as it learns from its mistakes and improves upon its overall success rate, say about 80 to 90 percent hits on targets, things should be okay.

WHAT NEXT

The Kargil war is over. But the proxy war that we have been fighting in Kashmir for last 10 years is far from over. If anything, it has been stepped up by Pakistan as indicated by the recent incidents such as militant's attack at the Srinagar cantonment. In fact, soon after the operations in Kargil were terminated, the Pakistani foreign minister was heard telling the BBC that there would be " ten more Kargils " if the Kashmir problem was not sorted out. We ought to take his statement seriously even if it's with a pinch of salt. But to ensure that we are never surprised again, we must get our act together and look beyond Kargil.

While it is imperative for India to equip itself with a high-end security system, the human factor is equally – if not more- relevant and important for future protection against Kargil-type intrusions.

All intelligence acquisition systems are broadly classified into two main heads: Human Intelligence (HUMINT) and Technical Intelligence (TECHINT). The latter can be divided into two distinct classes viz. Imagery Intelligence (IMINT) and Signal Intelligence (SIGINT). These again can be further sub-divided into land based systems like Electronic Fighting Vehicles Systems capable of providing electronic Support Measures (ESM), Electronic Counter Measures (ECM), Communication Intelligence (COMINT), Electronic Intelligence (ELINT) and the airborne systems such as the Unarmed Arial Vehicles (UAV), Joint Surveillance and Target Attack Radar System (JSTARS), Advanced Tactical Air Reconnaissance Systems (ATAR) and the Satellites. Technical jargon apart, what all this simply means is that information can either be acquired by men - and women of course – or by machines.

Let us first see what role the machines, or rather technology, can play in the intelligence wars of today and maybe tomorrow.

Hi Tech Intelligence

The Indian Army in Kargil lacked proper battlefield surveillance equipment. The Infantry man was dependent on second generation night vision goggles and obsolete devices such as BSFR Mark 1 (Battle Field Surveillance Radar) which can hardly discern enemy movement beyond half a kilometer or so.

Efforts are now on to procure medium range radars capable of detecting enemy movement up to 10 kilometers and the obsolete night vision goggles/ binoculars are being replaced with the latest thermal imaging devices that can detect intruders several kilometers away[24].

Plans are also afoot to acquire UAVs and other state of the art surveillance and communication equipment that will enhance our intelligence acquisition capability. Better late than never? The cliché notwithstanding, the point is that it is not as if we were unaware of these technologies before Kargil happened to us. In fact, the hi-tech equipment that is now being considered for import, has been part of the army's shopping list for long. So why the delay, one may ask. Some defence analysts and most bureaucrats have put the blame squarely on our limited defence budget. They say the cost of maintaining the massive manpower of the armed forces, leaves very little – not more than 10 percent or so – for modernization of weapons and equipment. According to them, the defence budget needs to be upped to at least 3 percent of the GDP if the requirements that have already been drawn are to be met.

While the government is likely to enhance the defence budget in the near future, things are not going to improve much unless we change our attitude.

Another facet of going all out in pursuit of high technology pertains to the dizzy advances made in the field of information technology (IT). This is one field where India could be a force to reckon with, as has already been proved by our private sector IT companies. The army too seems to have latched on to the ubiquitous microchip and has started thinking in terms of not so futuristic cyber wars where in surveillance will be based on satellites, UAV and battlefield radar's capable of tracking the enemy beyond visual range thousands of kilometers across the battle field. Satellite phones, fax and the Internet will all form part of the defence communication grid.

Human Intelligence

Many defence analysts are of the opinion that in the 21st century, Techint will surely replace humint. IT, Artificial Intelligence (AI), Visual Reality(VR) and enhanced reality (ER) will give a new meaning to intelligence and will accord it the capability to analyze the intangibles such as feelings, mindsets and intentions. It is said that as technology leaps forward, it will replace human intellect in many ways and with ER, techint will acquire a new face and emerge as one of the most sought after intellectual pursuits. Technology has an edge over human brain as far as things like memory, storage and easy recall are concerned but to say that it will soon replace human intellect is stretching things a bit too far. Technology no doubt can provide the end user with a plethora of operational and intelligence related inputs at the press of a computer key or by merely clicking at the mouse, but can it provide the commander in the field say an infantry battalion commander, with real time information during operations that his well trained reconnaissance parties can? Despite tremendous progress made in IT of late, is there any software presently available which can tell the commander anything about the state of morale of his troops or give him a feel of the pulse of his command? A computer can display the enemy's strength and general dispositions but what about his state of leadership, determination and drive? Only one computer is capable of analyzing all this, the human brain. Technology, or to be precise the IT as such can only augment the human effort by carrying out some mechanical functions but it can not replace the human brain, not in the foreseeable future at least.

CIA's inability to predict Pokharan II is considered as one of its biggest intelligence failures. If there is any intelligence agency in the world that has all imaginable – and unimaginable - marvels of technology at its disposal, it's the CIA. As a matter of fact, the Pokharan test ranges were kept under constant surveillance for over four years by CIA's billion dollar spies in the sky that could possibly read out the time from a wrist watch of the Indian soldier far below on the ground. And yet the world's most powerful and hi-tech secret service was so easily deceived by the Indian Army and other key players involved in the conduct of the most secret nuclear explosion. It was a victory of human intellect over technology indeed.

Integration is the key

In the corporate world its called M&A, that is merger and acquisition, where two or more companies join hands and integrate their resources and efforts to deal with the challenge posed by their competitors. Our intelligence services also need to integrate their activities if they are to succeed in facing the challenges posed by our adversaries. The strength of ISI lies in its being the sole agency that runs the intelligence machine of Pakistan and as such does not face the problems of lack of coordination and one-upmanship that our own intelligence agencies do. While it is neither feasible nor desirable – omnipotent organizations such as ISI pose dangerous pitfalls – to roll all our intelligence agencies into one a la the ISI, it is essential to integrate their overall effort in a more competent and homogeneous manner than being done at present. One way of doing this is to give more teeth to the JIC by providing it with regulatory authority so that its writ prevails over the entire intelligence community. There is also a need to set up a Joint Civil-Military intelligence organization tailor made for LICO. Also, cross attachment of Int Corps officers to civil agencies and vice versa on fixed tenure basis will also go a long way in inculcating better understanding of each other's constraints, problems and prospects.

The two main systems of intelligence acquisition, humint and techint need integration too, since both are important and are in fact complementary to each other.

Besides, with the growing complexity of techint, we need to work towards systems integration of various communication links such as computers, databases and satellites.

There is also a strong case for integrating the country's defence R&D with civil R&D to encourage competitiveness free control and intellectual simulation in the technical field. As a matter of fact, for best results, we must ensure integration of the entire process of research, development, production and procurement of defence requirements.

Though there has been much talk of integrating all three-service headquarters with the defence ministry, the idea is yet to be executed on ground. And it is not only the bureaucrats who for obvious reasons have shown reluctance to implement this long-standing proposal; difference of opinion exists even among the services in this regard. Needless to say, unless the three Chiefs of Staff follow an integrated approach in advising the government on matters military, nothing worthwhile will be achieved in integrating their headquarters with the Ministry of Defence. It will also be prudent for all out political parties not to indulge in politicking but to adopt an integrated stance while deciding issues pertaining to the country's defence.

In short, integration is the name of the game. An integrated thinking is a must if we are to out think our adversary who is contemplating ten more Kargils. Even though it sounds like a hollow threat, knowing the ways of military leaders in Pakistan, possibility of another conflict can never be ruled out. But the next encounter, hopefully, will not be an unexpected one.

In Conclusion

The Kargil war has amply brought into focus the weaknesses in our intelligence systems—the collection, coordination, collation, analysis and timely dissemination and decision making by the authorities to act on its basis. The armed forces despite the initial hiccups reacted boldly and bravely and the media ofcourse played a pivotal role in bringing about awareness real time to the nation and in providing suitable perception to the outside world. The role of air force in Mountainous terrain needs to be researched so that this important and expensive service can play a meaningfull role in such situation. National Secuity council needs to come in place to take some vital decision relating to national security and ofcourse the intelligence system needs to be revamped. The Subramaniam committee once finalised should form the basis of rectifying failures at various levels.

Notes

Notes

Notes